"Greg Cohen makes a compelling [...] product managers and offers ke[...] marketplace. It is a must read for any product manager looking to make the change."
Gina Han, Senior Product Manager, Intuit

"This is an outstanding book. With insight and clarity, Greg Cohen shows the 'hows' and 'whys' of Agile product management. It is an essential guide for any Agile team member—even if not a product manager. 'Agile Excellence™ for Product Managers' will help teams focus effort where it really counts."
Therese Padilla, President, AIPMM (Association of International Product Marketing and Management)

"There are plenty of books that explain Agile, but they are mostly from the development point of view. 'Agile Excellence™ for Product Managers' provides the unique perspective of how product management professionals fit into the Agile framework and describes how Agile and product management fit together. Cohen provides a comprehensive treatise on being an Agile product manager."
Ivan Chalif, Director of Product Marketing at Alterian and Chief Blogger at TheProductologist.com

"If making the move to Agile seems daunting, then read this book. Greg Cohen lays out the necessary steps to succeed with Agile."
Anar Taori, Senior Product Manager, VMware

"This book is invaluable for any product manager looking to learn how to fully leverage Agile development to create better products faster."
Bob Hsiung, Development Manager at MIT Media Lab

"If you're a product manager and deal with software projects of any kind, Agile development methods are the key to being able to compete in the 21st century. Agile can ensure you and your company remain adaptable to shifting market conditions and deliver the right product, to the right customer, at the right time. If you use or are planning to use Agile methods, then 'Agile Excellence™ for Product Managers' is a must-read guide to help you maximize your success."
Bill Takacs, Director Product Management, Gear6

"This book is a treasure chest of practical advice on working with Agile teams that can be immediately applied."
Jeff Smith, VP Solutions, Vizu

"Today's companies need to be responsive to market opportunities, competitive dynamics, and customer needs. Agile methods can help get you there, and this book shows you how."
Dave Karel, Vice President Product Marketing, SuccessFactors

Agile Excellence™ for Product Managers

A Guide to Creating Winning Products with Agile Development Teams

By Greg Cohen

E-mail: info@superstarpress.com
20660 Stevens Creek Blvd., Suite 210
Cupertino, CA 95014

Copyright © 2010 by Greg Cohen

All rights reserved. No patent liability is assumed with respect to the use of the information contained herein. Although every precaution has been taken in the preparation of this book, the publisher and author assume no responsibility for errors or omissions. Neither is any liability assumed for damages resulting from the use of the information contained herein.

First Printing: February 2010
Paperback ISBN: 978-1-60773-074-3 (1-60773-074-X)
Place of Publication: Silicon Valley, California, USA
Paperback Library of Congress Number: 2009944085

eBook ISBN: 978-1-60773-075-0 (1-60773-075-8)

Trademarks

All terms mentioned in this book that are known to be trademarks or service marks have been appropriately capitalized. Super Star Press™ cannot attest to the accuracy of this information. Use of a term in this book should not be regarded as affecting the validity of any trademark or service mark.

Warning and Disclaimer

Every effort has been made to make this book as complete and as accurate as possible, but no warranty of fitness is implied. The information provided is on an "as is" basis. The authors and the publisher shall have neither liability nor responsibility to any person or entity with respect to any loss or damages arising from the information contained in this book.

Dedication

To my loving wife, children, brother, and parents. As a product manager, it has been a challenge for me to explain what I really do for a living; maybe this book will provide some clarity. Thank you for your unconditional support over the years.

Acknowledgments

I owe a great debt to many friends, colleagues, practitioners, and experts who have contributed to my thinking over the past fifteen years. Although it would be impossible to list everyone, there are a number who stand out in my memory and deserve mention.

To Jeff Bay, who in 2001 introduced me to Kent Beck's ideas and first opened my eyes to an alternate way of doing things. To Bill Gross, Scott Weisse, Scott Banister, Brian Steele, Bob Kavner, and Michael Feldman at IdeaLab!, where rapid iteration, flexibility, and experimentation were encouraged. To Joe Arnold and Ken Branson, who have deepened my understanding of Agile methods and been a sounding board throughout the writing of this book. To Ken Schwaber and Mike Beedle, who so effectively communicated the rationale for Scrum. To Tom DeMarco, who made me think about ways to manage risk in software development. To Mike Cohn, for his methods on writing user stories. To Ryan Shriver, for his contributions on defining system qualities. To Mary and Tom Poppendieck, Corey Ladas, and Karl Scotland, for their work on Lean and Kanban. To Marty Cagan, who always questions the *status quo* in product management. To David Finke, Geoff Huckleberry, Ross Merritt, Anant Chintamaneni, Richard Bateman, Steven Drucker, Jack Greene, Kurt Ishiaka, Xinmin Wang, and Peter Doan, who kept it real as I continued to hone my thinking. To Susan Wheeler, who gave me a chance to prove myself. To Brian Lawley, Rich Mironov, Sridhar Ramanathan, and John Konsin, who have inspired me and been invaluable mentors on my professional journey.

Lastly to my colleagues on the Silicon Valley Product Management Association (SVPMA) Board, the membership, and the many speakers who have come to share their experiences on a monthly basis since 2000.

Thanks to my reviewers Jeff Bay, Tom Belote, Peter Doan, Ross Merritt, and Susan Wheeler, who suffered through early drafts and invested precious hours and energy helping me refine my thinking and presentation. Thank you to my editors Bill Hilton and Deneene Bell for making this book more readable, to Liz Tadman for keeping this project on track, to Delia Colaco and Reshma Tendulkar for their work on layout, to Yasemin Akyuz for cover design and illustrations, and to Mitchell Levy for believing in this book. And a special thanks to Brian Lawley, without whose encouragement this book may not have been written.

A Message From Super Star Press™

Thank you for your purchase of this Super Star Press book. It is available online at http://happyabout.info/agileproductmangers.php or at other online and physical bookstores.

- Please contact us for quantity discounts at sales@happyabout.info
- If you want to be informed by email of upcoming Happy About® books, please email bookupdate@happyabout.info

Happy About is interested in you if you are an author who would like to submit a non-fiction book proposal or a corporation that would like to have a book written for you. Please contact us by email editorial@happyabout.info or phone (1-408-257-3000).

Other Happy About books available include:

- Expert Product Management:
  http://happyabout.info/expertproductmanagement.php
- Expert Product Management Toolkit Bundle:
  http://happyabout.info/expertproductmanagement.php
- The Phenomenal Product Manager:
  http://happyabout.info/phenomenal-product-manager.php
- Get Out of the Way:
  http://happyabout.info/getoutoftheway.php
- Scrappy Project Managment:
  http://happyabout.info/scrappyabout/project-management.php
- 42 Rules™ of Employee Engagement:
  http://happyabout.info/42rules/employee-engagement.php
- 42 Rules for Successful Collaboration:
  http://www.happyabout.info/42rules/successful-collaboration.php
- 42 Rules™ to Jumpstart Your Professional Success:
  http://happyabout.info/42rules/jumpstartprofessionalservices.php
- I'm on LinkedIn—Now What???:
  http://happyabout.info/linkedinhelp.php
- Twitter Means Business:
  http://happyabout.info/twitter/tweet2success.php
- Blitz the Ladder:
  http://happyabout.info/blitz.php
- The Successful Introvert:
  http://happyabout.info/thesuccessfulintrovert.php
- Happy About an Extra Hour Every Day:
  http://happyabout.info/an-extra-hour.php

Contents

Foreword by Brian Lawley

As product managers, our jobs can be very hectic. There are always too many things to do, multiple competing priorities, and a wide variety of constituents that want our attention and time. Making sure that everything for our products is in place so that the products succeed and customers are happy can be a daunting job. While juggling all of these responsibilities, we also have to determine what the right requirements and priorities are to guide our development teams. This means spending quality time with customers, tracking the competition, monitoring trends, and gathering information from our sales, support, operations, and other departments.

With all of this responsibility, it seems a little intimidating to have to learn a new way of working with our teams. Yet of all of the changes and improvements that have occurred in the product management profession over the years, perhaps none have had as much of an impact as Agile development methodologies. As Agile development is being rapidly adopted (and, in many cases, mandated) by engineering, we have to adapt our profession to it. And we need to learn new skills to be successful.

The good news is that Agile can make product management a more rewarding job. It can help you get valuable new features to customers in a rapid manner. It can help air issues with your team and get them quickly resolved. It can make your teams more accountable. And it can help you increase your focus on building great products that your customers love.

The other good news is that making the transition to Agile (or becoming better at it if you are already doing it) is not nearly as difficult as it might seem. This book will give you the knowledge and insight you need to get you there.

Brian Lawley
CEO & Founder, 280 Group
Author, 'Expert Product Management' and
'The Phenomenal Product Manager'
November 2009

Preface

This book is written for product managers who are making the transition to working with Agile development teams, as well as for Product Owners and project managers looking for better ways to organize and lead in their companies. I have tried to describe Agile through the lens of product management, including how Agile helps deliver winning products to market. Although what follows does not require an advanced understanding of product management, it is assumed the reader has basic product management skills. Also, because this book is intended for product managers, I have kept it as brief—and as practical—as possible. I know you are busy, and stretched by many competing objectives. My goal is that you can read this book in a single sitting on a three-hour flight to visit a customer.

When I was first introduced to Agile in 2001, it was a liberating experience. It freed me to be a better product manager. I was able to manage risk and adapt to emerging requirements at an entirely new level of effectiveness and do so in a way that was not disruptive or demoralizing to the development team. It was one the happiest moments in my career. Although at that stage I did not understand the theories behind it, I realized that Agile was a better way to develop software for the customer, the company, and the employees. Later, as I learned more about the theoretical underpinnings, it became increasingly clear why traditional, serial, software development just did not work that well.

In the pages that follow, I hope to impart some of the initial excitement I felt when I first started using Agile, and share with you its fundamentals from a product management perspective so that you can support your team, be in control of your product, and realize immediate benefits. I also hope that, by knowing what to expect from Agile, you will be able to identify if your team is underperforming and facilitate change to unblock them.

This book takes the reader on a journey that starts 10,000 feet in the air, with an overview of how an Agile development team works, and then makes a circling descent to reveal increasing detail of how product managers work within an Agile development environment. We finally land in Chapter 6, with a step-by-step guide to getting started and succeeding with Agile. Important concepts are touched upon two to three times from different angles to allow the reader to acquire a deeper appreciation of how they fit in with the whole.

The book is divided into nine chapters. In Chapter 1, we will define Agile development, understand its principles, look at why it works, and, most importantly, explain why it is good for you as a product manager. In Chapter 2, we will look at Scrum, a popular Agile method, in some depth. In Chapters 3, 4, and 5 we will look at the mechanics of Agile from the product manager's perspective and use Scrum as an example. We will cover how you manage a release, how you plan for a release, and how the documentation that you provide to your team changes. In Chapter 6, we will go through a step-by-step view of everything you need to put in place to get started and be successful with Agile, including how you interface with marketing and sales.

Chapter 7 covers how teams generally organize around Agile and identifies obstacles to team performance. Chapter 8 explores XP (Extreme Programming) and Lean Software Development methods to provide a broader understanding of Agile in practice. Regardless of the methodology your team selects, it is important to adapt it to support your products and customers while also working within your company's culture and your team's skill set. This chapter is intended to help you understand different ways to implement Agile. Chapter 9 concludes with a discussion of how Agile can assist with company-wide process improvement; the methods best suited for different types of projects; and a review of the key points of the earlier chapters.

It would be easy for a reader to think this book advocates Scrum over other Agile methods because of the time devoted to it. This is not the case, and the book tries to remain agnostic while providing a solid foundation for any Agile method with which you might work. Of the three methods described in this book (Scrum, XP, and Lean), I had to select one to carry through from start to finish. Scrum is best suited for this purpose because of its rigid definition around process, and its openness around development methodologies. Scrum also has a well-defined role for the product manager, also known as the Product Owner, which covers responsibilities and methods of interfacing with the development team. After completing this book, you should be able to pick up and work with any Agile methodology.

I hope that you will enjoy this book and come to experience the same satisfaction I have had working with Agile teams. Furthermore, I hope that through your hard work and the help of Agile, you will deliver greater value to your customers, more quickly than ever before. Lastly, I hope that you will view this book as one of the waypoints on your journey of continuous improvement. Our development teams, our companies, and we as product managers, must never give up the perfectionist pursuit of building better software to satisfy our customers.

1 Why Agile Is Good for Product Management

Agile is often introduced to an organization through a development team seeking to deliver better software, faster. The change, however, sometimes causes anxiety to product managers. If this describes you, your anxiety is unfounded. Your development team wants to improve how they deliver software, and it would be foolish to do anything less than encourage them and jump right in to help. Agile is one of the best developments to ever happen to product management and our ability to deliver products that customers love.

Traditional Software Development

Before we look at Agile, let's initially take a look at the traditional software product development process (Figure 1.1). First, a company must consider all products in which it might invest, a process otherwise known as ideation. Next the company screens each idea for fit and potential return on investment. An idea that passes the screening is further defined, designed, coded, and tested. This phase is often known as "waterfall development" because the team moves through the four stages of define, design, code, and test in a serial fashion, completing one stage before starting the next. When that process is complete, the product is typically deployed to a limited customer set for beta testing, which confirms that the product works as designed and without unintended consequences. Usually issues are uncovered in beta testing, but only the most severe get addressed, because each change adds the risk of introducing new bugs to the system and delays the delivery of the product. Once out of beta, the product is made available for production use. At each step in this process, there are decisions or stage gates, where the company evaluates whether the product is progressing as planned and whether the investment still makes sense based on the latest information. Depending on the company, these gates can be formal steps with written approvals, or less formal check-ins.

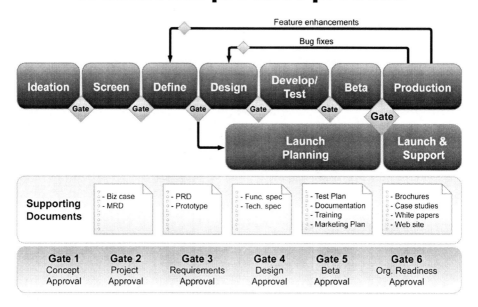

Figure 1.1: The traditional software product development process

Once the product clears the definition stage, it has a high probability of making it to production. Enough due diligence has occurred for the company to feel confident that it understands the market problem, market opportunity, what the product needs to do, and the investment needed to take the product to market. Thus, as the product enters the design stage, launch planning occurs in parallel to development to establish the product's positioning, messaging, and internal and external communications plans.

At the different stages, documents are created to support each process. These include a business case analysis, market requirements document, product re-quirements document, test plan, and collateral. The documents are used to dis-seminate market and product information within the team and company, capture decisions, and improve decision-making.

The product manager plays a central role in moving products through all these stages. She works closely with the different departments to make sure the product is delivered on time and to specification. She also ensures the other departments are trained and ready to support the product. Ultimately, the product manager is responsible for the commercial success of the product.

The Cost of Change

I was taught it was fairly inexpensive to make changes to a project early in the traditional development process—for example in the definition or design phases—but very expensive once development proper began, and exponentially more expensive as the product entered testing and production (Figure 1.2). This advice was reinforced by actual experience.

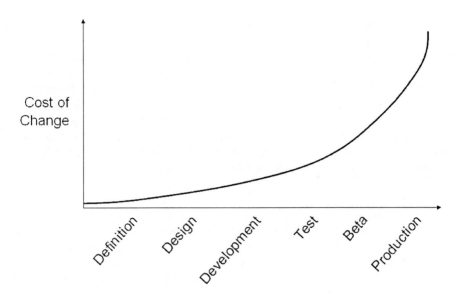

Figure 1.2: The cost of change for a traditional software project

When I introduced changes to a product during the development stage because of new information or a new customer requirement, a domino effect of negative consequences followed. First, the process had to go through formal change control that was intended to ensure everyone on the team, especially those handling development and QA, understood the change and that the plan of record was kept up-to-date. This meant documentation and meetings. Second, the effort had to be estimated and, often, the schedule recast.

Assessing the effort needed to develop a complex feature was hard; gauging that feature's impact on the schedule was near impossible. It also became clear that these changes caused the development team a significant amount of redesign and rework that, under the pressure of a tight schedule, was demoralizing.

Because change was so expensive in the later stages of the project, I invested a lot of time and energy in gathering requirements and getting the definition right. I also speculated about the future needs of the system. That way, even if the functionality would not be delivered in the early releases of the product, the foundation would be there to support it. Additionally, in the back of my mind, I could never let go of the idea that the second release would not be for six to nine months after the first one. If I thought a customer would need a feature in that time frame, I felt obliged to add it to the release even if there was no conclusive evidence of a need for it.

The implications of this exponential cost curve are severe. First, it is challenging to get everything right up front. Users do not always know what they want, nor is it their job to know. Even with study and prototypes, it is nearly impossible to ferret out all possible use situations until the product is deployed in a live environment and used in the context of a real customer's day. Further, as I highlighted in the previous paragraph, attempting to do so promotes bad decision-making and poor habits on the part of the product manager, including speculation (about what the product will need to do) and hedging (by adding extra, partially researched features). Lastly, even if the product manager could define the product perfectly to start with, markets are dynamic—over the six to eighteen months it takes to finish a release, the target will move.

Kent Beck, who developed Extreme Programming, asks a very thought-provoking question: if our cost curve were relatively flat (Figure 1.3) would we behave differently? Would we delay decisions until we had better information? Would we over-design in anticipation of future needs or just design and build to our current requirement? Would we be able to deliver more value to the market, and would we be able to deliver better software faster? Agile attempts to change the cost of change equation.[1]

---

1. Kent Beck, *Extreme Programming Explained: Embrace Change* (Indianapolis: Addison-Wesley, 2000), 21–24.

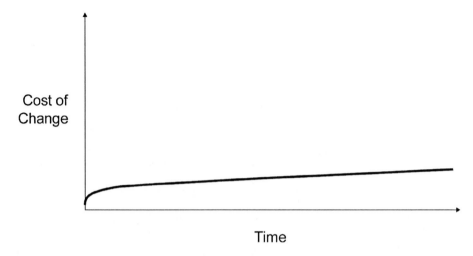

Cost of Change

Time

Figure 1.3: *The cost of change during a project with a flat cost curve*

Agile Software Development

Agile development is an alternate way to build products. Instead of following a linear path to define, design, develop, and test the software, Agile delivers functionality through more frequent and smaller iterations (Figure 1.4). Large requirements are developed over multiple iterations and developed in small "vertical" slices of functionality. Each slice is limited in its capabilities, but works end to end, including the graphical user interface (GUI), application logic, and the database. Each slice must deliver business value. This differs from the traditional approach, which might look to develop in "horizontal" slices by designing and developing the data, logic, and interface tiers up front and integrating them late in the project, or by developing the entire data tier first and then building the application on top of it. In the traditional approach, business value is often only realized at the end of the project when the software components are integrated.

Although Agile development changes the way a product is developed, it does not change the need for sound product management. The company still needs a good up-front process to prioritize which ideas get funded. The company also needs to position and differentiate its product in the marketplace. Thus, the fundamental role of the product manager—to be the voice of the customer in development and ensure the right product is built—remains intact. But, with Agile, it is now possible to respond more quickly to the marketplace and deliver a higher quality product, sooner.

Agile product process

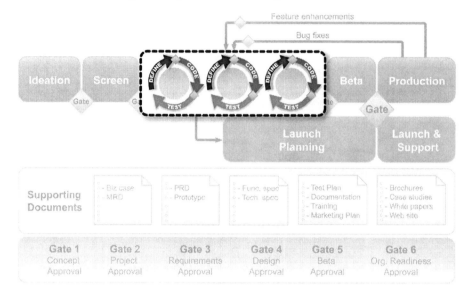

Figure 1.4: Agile software development creates products through multiple, small iterations.

Further, although the software is built through a series of small iterations, this does not in itself change the release cycle. If a company normally releases every six months, the company may choose to maintain that release schedule after implementing Agile. The difference is that it would develop the release in small iterations, for example, by combining six monthly iteration cycles. You should examine, however, whether your customers would prefer faster, smaller increments, or larger, less frequent releases. For example, if you currently release annually, could you instead release quarterly, accelerating value to your customers and making your product more competitive in the sales cycle?

If you use your Agility to release more often, your launch planning will need to adjust to accommodate the increased cadence. You may choose to shorten your beta programs or conduct them entirely differently. Web services companies often deploy betas directly on their live sites and expose a sub-segment of unsuspecting users to it. Others ask users to opt-in to using the new version. In addition to betas, documentation also changes, as well as how product management interfaces with development.

What's in It for You?

Why is changing to Agile development good for product managers? "What's in it for me?" you ask. There are three high-level reasons why product managers directly benefit from working with Agile teams:

- Greater **visibility** into the progress of a release, as you track your project through actual working software rather than status reports

- More **flexibility** to deal with changes during the development of a release, as priorities can be adjusted before each iteration

- Higher **quality** plus shorter QA cycles (on one project where I adopted Agile, QA shrunk from two weeks to four hours)

The increase in quality comes as a result of three measures that are ongoing throughout the development: automated unit testing, frequent integration, and acceptance testing. As a result of the automated unit tests, late changes and production-issue fixes become less risky. You can expect to experience new levels of confidence in your product and avoid the long delays associated with manual regression testing.

You will not just have visibility into the progress of a release but also greater transparency into the trade-offs regarding changes you make. When combined with the added flexibility from developing in short iterations, you will be able to more easily accommodate changing priorities and make better-informed decisions.

In the end, you will be able to build more of the right products, deliver them to the market sooner, and achieve superior results (and have more fun while you do it!).

Why Now?

Interestingly, Agile is not new. In fact it has been around since the 1990s. It is worth asking: Why now? Why has Agile become so popular?

To be a little controversial, I would say it is because of the failure of traditional serial or "waterfall" development and our attempts to control the software development process. Although I know there are many advocates of waterfall, in my experience it just does not work that well. Further, the Internet and globalization have had profound effects on the software industry, increasing the intensity of competition and the rate of change. If you are still releasing annually or over an 18-month cycle, by the time your next version is available, the market will have moved. Further, with the advent of Software-as-a-Service, hosted models, hosted download, and self-updating software, releases can occur with much greater frequency. Thus, companies have looked for a better way to develop software. Agile has met the challenge. Even so, best practices for Agile continue to evolve, including the constant challenge of working with distributed teams across multiple time zones.

The Agile Manifesto

In 2001, seventeen Agile pioneers[2] gathered at Snowbird Ski Resort in Utah to discuss common themes. The group captured its deepest beliefs in the "Manifesto for Agile Software Development":

We are uncovering better ways of developing

software by doing it and helping others do it.

Through this work we have come to value:

Individuals and interactions *over processes and tools*

Working software *over comprehensive documentation*

Customer collaboration *over contract negotiation*

Responding to change *over following a plan*

That is, while there is value in the items on

the right, we value the items on the left more.[3]

As you reflect on the meaning of the manifesto, it is worth noting that a lot of early software product development techniques were developed within IT and in the context of custom software development. So customer collaboration means collaborating with whoever represents the customer within your

---

2. Kent Beck, Mike Beedle, Arie van Bennekum, Alistair Cockburn, Ward Cunningham, Martin Fowler, James Grenning, Jim Highsmith, Andrew Hunt, Ron Jeffries, Jon Kern, Brian Marick, Robert C. Martin, Steve Mellor, Ken Schwaber, Jeff Sutherland, and Dave Thomas.

3. http://agilemanifesto.org/

organization. In commercial software development, the product manager (or sometimes a business analyst) is usually the proxy for the customer, representing their interests within the development process.

We in product management must also commit to the Agile Manifesto. As we look to embrace these values, we must understand how it effects our actions and how we carry out our responsibilities. Let's take a more detailed look at the four main principles of the Agile Manifesto:

Individuals and Interaction—Creating great products is purely a human endeavor. Identifying and understanding a customer problem, applying technology and design to a solution, and generating awareness of the solution is hard work. There are guidelines but no recipes for success. Further, the task is beyond the means of any single individual. Rather it requires a team of experienced professionals working in concert. Process can help ensure important steps are not missed, but it will never substitute for the judgment that each team member applies to thousands of decisions during the project. Good decisions emerge from teams whose members are aligned, honest with each other, and in which each member holds the team goal above his personal ambition. The product manager is central to maintaining a cohesive team with singular purpose. Towards this end, the product manager must foster an environment that respects the opinions, contributions, and individuality of each team member and where open and meaningful dialogue can occur.

Working Software—Our objective as product managers is to produce products that delight customers and solve a real need. Documentation can assist in achieving this goal, but documentation itself is not the goal. I know that I have not always held true to this value. I have been guilty of hiding behind documentation to deflect blame during a development project. If something were not coded as specified in the requirement, I would look incredulous and say, "I don't know how it was missed—it's right here on page 164 of the Product Requirements Document!" No doubt part of this reaction had to do with my insecurities as a young product manager, but it also had to do with the black box of development. This is not to say that the team members were hiding anything from me, or were not willing to show me what they had developed. It was just that integration rarely happened until the later stages of the project. The team did not have anything that it could show me or that I could interact with myself. I had no way of knowing if a requirement was poorly worded, misunderstood, or just missed entirely, until close to the end of the project. Further, being able to point to where the botched requirement was documented was of little consolation, because *we as a team had failed*: we missed an opportunity to improve our product in the eyes of the customer. Fortunately, Agile solves this problem with the frequent release of working software that provides a reference for meaningful conversation.

Customer Collaboration—In traditional serial software development, requirements and specifications documents are often signed off by the team and the product manager or by the company and the customer. Any scope change requires additional negotiation, trade-offs, and, possibly, increased fees. This creates a confrontational environment that prioritizes stability over building the right product. Thus, developing to the agreed plan may ensure contract compliance, but will not produce satisfied customers or users. Contract compliance is a short-term goal that requires the unrealistic effort of trying to define a product entirely up front. Acquiring satisfied customers who will give good references is the long-term goal, and it means working with the customer to understand what is needed, then working with the development team to understand what is possible.

Responding to Change—As product managers, we invest time talking to customers about their needs, observing them using our products, or solving their problems without our products; in addition, we validate concepts, prototypes, and software in pre-release form. At each stage of discovery, customers acquire new levels of understanding about our design intent, and we learn new lessons. We know changes will be necessary, and, therefore, we need to adjust our practices to accommodate change at all stages of the product development process. As in the case with contract compliance, above, following the plan is not the goal. Rather, our goal is working software that solves customers' problems, and maybe even delights them with its utility.

Post a copy of the Agile Manifesto on your wall and in your meeting rooms. If you find yourself or your team slipping back into old patterns, look at it again. The values embodied in these principles will keep your team grounded and moving in the right direction.

The Common Threads of Agile

Agile software development is not a single methodology but rather a development philosophy or approach. Many different methodologies fit under the Agile umbrella, including Scrum, Extreme Programming, Dynamic Systems Development Method, Feature Driven Development, Agile Unified Process, and many more. Common themes include:

- Development in short iterations or time boxes that typically last from one to four weeks

- Responsibility by the team during each iteration for the full software development cycle, including planning, requirements definition, analysis, design, coding, unit testing, and acceptance testing, at which point the product is demonstrated to its stakeholders

- Disciplined project management

- Frequent inspection and adjustment

- Collaboration between self-organizing, cross-functional teams

- Emphasis on customer needs

Agile techniques minimize overall project risk, and let the product adapt to change very quickly. At the end of each iteration, the product should be functional and able to be released. The product manager, however, may decide to combine multiple iterations to have enough new functionality to warrant a market release.

Why Agile Works

Agile works because it supports the process of software development in four key areas:

1. Empirical process
2. Daily visibility
3. Socialization of information
4. Rapid feedback cycles

Empirical Process

It is easier to understand an empirical process by first looking at a defined process. A defined process is one in which defined inputs generate defined outputs. This is the original manufacturing model. It is repeatable, and it is the model that traditional software development has assumed (Figure 1.5).

If I take a blueprint to any machine shop around the world, I can expect to get matching products back from all the shops. The blueprint specifies the material, the dimensions, and tolerances. The actual cutting paths may differ, but the end product will largely be the same. However, if I take a product requirements document and give that to ten different development teams, the resultant code bases may perform similar functions, but the products will probably look and behave differently and optimize along different dimensions. Further, the lines of code will be different and the programming language may be different. It would be a little like asking two journalists to cover the same story: although the facts of the resulting reports should be the same, the styles and perspectives will be different.

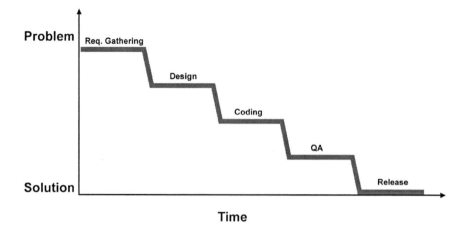

Figure 1.5: *Traditional software development assumes a defined process.*

In contrast, the empirical process is nonlinear. It requires frequent inspection and adjustment. It is well suited for new product development, which requires research and creativity—both relatively unpredictable activities. Software development, including the product management step of requirements gathering and validation, is best suited to an empirical model.[4]

Software development teams are always creating something new. They do not follow a straight path with a defined output that is the same each time they go through the process. Instead, teams cycle through knowledge creation and problem solving (Figure 1.6). As team members formulate the solution, new questions emerge and new requirements need to be gathered. Occasionally the team has to restart. An assumption turns out to be false, such as the availability of complete and accurate data to drive a critical process. Sometimes the environment changes and a new technology emerges that needs to be supported. At times the solution functionally works but the performance is slow. Further, there is no escaping the QA team, whom you can always count on to identify some good issues that need solving. The list goes on. To accommodate this, the team must frequently check its progress and adjust its plan.[5]

---

4. Ken Schwaber and Mike Beedle, *Agile Software Development with Scrum* (New Jersey: Prentice Hall, 2002), 24–25 and 106–108.

5. Steve Tennant, "Create Better Products with a Structured Process for Collaboration," (presented at the second annual Silicon Valley P-Camp for Product Managers, Sunnyvale, California, March 14, 2009).

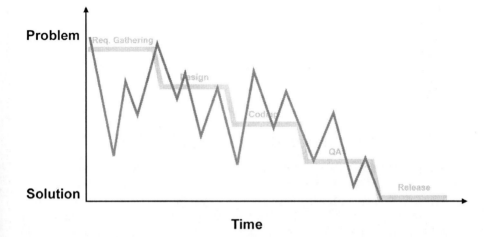

Figure 1.6: Software development follows an empirical process that is similar to new product development.

Daily Visibility

Agile improves visibility into the development process with a daily standup meeting. At the meeting, team members let each other know what they are working on and if they need help. Roadblocks are explicitly called out. Because this meeting is daily, issues cannot be ignored. Further, each developer commits to what she will be working on next in front of the team. Through this process, the team develops trust and the ability to be open and honest.

Socialization of Information

Agile processes facilitate the socialization of information. First, as mentioned above, the daily standup drives trust in the team. This creates an environment conducive to sharing news, even if it is discouraging. Secondly, because team members meet daily to share their accomplishments and plans, individual knowledge quickly becomes team knowledge, and the team stays aligned.[6]

Rapid Feedback Cycles

Rapid feedback cycles are embedded in the Agile process. The feedback loop accelerates the team's learning and supports the empirical process needed in software development. There are three connected cycles: the release, the

---

6. Schwaber and Beedle, *Agile Software Development with Scrum*, 111–113.

iteration, and daily standup. The release may be an extended cycle, but the iteration is one to four weeks, and the daily standup provides feedback every twenty-four hours. Agile feedback loops share much in common with the Plan, Do, Check, and Adjust (PDCA) process popularized by Dr. W. Edwards Deming in his quality control work: the team members formulate a course of action, execute against it, inspect their progress, and adjust their course accordingly.

Product Management Just Got Better

Returning to the main topic of this chapter, what does Agile mean for you as a product manager? It means your job isn't changing, but your ability to perform your job well has dramatically improved. Everything you should be doing as a product manager is still intact, including conducting market and customer research, creating personas and business cases, making tough trade-offs and prioritizations, planning roadmaps, developing pricing, creating sales tools, and launching the product. But with Agile, you can get feedback faster, incorporate research findings earlier, and adjust your plan sooner. You can expect to deliver better products, with richer features and fewer bugs, to your customers. Plus, you can reduce your time to market and accelerate revenue for your product.

Of course, you will need to change parts of your process to support the development team and leverage the benefits of Agile. This will be covered in the remaining chapters of this book. So get set as we first look at Scrum as an example of an Agile development methodology and then explore release management, release planning, documentation, and everything else you need to know to achieve *Agile Excellence*.

2 Understanding Scrum

We're going to use Scrum as our first example of an Agile method because it is widely used and highly structured. Regardless of the methodology that your company selects, the same Agile principles apply. In this chapter, and throughout the book, I will introduce both general Agile terms (such as "an iteration") and the corresponding Scrum terminology (which, in that instance, would be "a Sprint"). Scrum-specific nomenclature has been capitalized for clarity. You should also adjust the chosen methodology to your organization, its culture, the types of problems you solve, and the individual skills of your team. Nevertheless, try to run as true as you can to the methodology you select for the first few iterations before tuning it for your situation. Otherwise, you may inadvertently discard beneficial practices.

Scrum was developed in the mid-1990s by Jeff Sutherland, Ken Schwaber, Mike Beedle and others. Sutherland invented many of the practices, Schwaber then formalized them for systems development, and Beedle wrapped in XP practices. Schwaber and Beedle further popularized Scrum in 2002 with their book 'Agile Software Development with Scrum.' The authors set out to create a methodology that supports an empirical process, as described in Chapter 1 of this book. Their goal was to realize a productivity boost of 100–300 percent, increase flexibility, lower risk, and create a better place to work. Much of the description of Scrum in this chapter is based on their book. I am grateful for their superb treatment of the topic and encourage all readers interested in learning more about Scrum to consult this source.

Overview of Scrum

Scrum is really a project management methodology. Requirements are maintained in a backlog, called the Product Backlog, prioritized by business value, which you see on the left hand side of Figure 2.1. The Product Backlog represents all work to be done on the product. This includes everything from customer requests, new features, usability enhancement, bug fixes, performance improvements, re-architecting, and so on.

Bird-eye view of Scrum

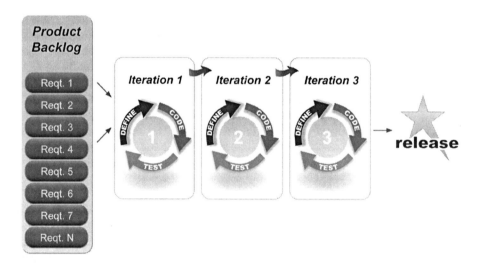

Figure 2.1: *Bird's-eye view of Scrum*

To the right of the Product Backlog are time boxes or iterations. In Scrum these are known as Sprints and usually last two to four weeks, depending on the product or service. Items are taken off the backlog in priority order to be worked on in the current iteration. The backlog can always be reprioritized at any time, but once a requirement is under development—meaning it has been placed into an iteration—it is no longer in the backlog and cannot be changed.

In Scrum, there exists a team position called the Product Owner. In commercial software development, the product manager usually assumes this role. The Product Owner manages the creation and prioritization of Product Backlog items. If product management has its ducks in a row, the backlog is well thought-out and maps the product vision and strategic goals of the company.

As requirements move towards the top of the Product Backlog, the Product Owner adds more detail to those requirements and the development team estimates the work effort that will be involved. Therefore, for items that are lower down in the list, it is okay to have placeholders such as "scalability" and "foreign language" support that might be very large requirements and need further definition. This way, the Product Owner can keep track of key requirements for the product and organize her own work effort using the Product Backlog. The requirement must then be fully defined to be included in a Sprint.

This simple backlog system and Agile's iterative approach makes for a powerful overall system that enables the team to move forward and learn from doing, testing, and sharing, rather than being sidelined waiting for 100 percent clarity of all the requirements in the release. To get started, a team only needs enough defined backlog items for the first iteration or Sprint. This provides time to further develop additional backlog items and details for the next Sprint. This is not an excuse to forego upfront requirement gathering—all Agile will do in those circumstances is let you get to the wrong answer faster. It can, however, let the team start moving forward on a project while still filling in detail.

For websites and hosted applications, an iteration can equal a release. For on-premise software or for Software-as-a-Service offerings where the user cannot quickly absorb change, releases combine multiple iterations and occur less frequently. Regardless of whether each Sprint is released at completion or combined into a larger release, each iteration should still *potentially* be shippable, meaning it is functional and tested.

An Iteration

An iteration typically lasts one to four weeks and has four distinct phases (Figure 2.2).

1. Planning
2. Development
3. Review
4. Retrospective

During the Planning phase, the Product Backlog items to be developed during the iteration are selected, and the goal of the iteration is formulated. During Development, each requirement selected for the iteration goes through definition, coding, and two types of testing. Automated unit tests are written to confirm the new code works as designed. The automated unit tests also ensure that "Requirement 2" does not break "Requirement 1" or anything else that came before it—an imperative for iterative development. Once unit testing is complete, acceptance or business testing occurs to confirm that the requirement meets the functional needs of the user.

During the Development phase there is also a daily status meeting known as the daily standup. In this meeting, each team member states what they did the previous day, what they are going to do today, and identifies any existing or foreseeable roadblocks. Issues are taken offline to be solved in other meetings.

When the iteration nears completion, a review meeting is held with all stake-holders to demonstrate the new software and receive feedback on it and the functionality that has been developed. The last phase, or Retrospective, is a postmortem for the team to discuss how the process could be improved.

Iteration

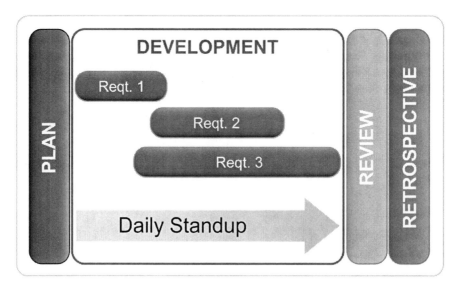

Figure 2.2: *An iteration or Sprint*

The Scrum Team

The Scrum Team commits to what will be achieved in the Sprint, and no one but the team can make that commitment. The team collectively owns analysis, design, coding, testing, and both internal and external documentation. Achieving the Sprint goal is a cross-functional effort by everyone on the team. Members will have titles within the company, but there are no titles marking hierarchy within the team. Members are expected to apply their full skill set and expertise to solve the problems. Teams are entirely self-organizing.

The Scrum Team members are the Scrum Master, the Product Owner, and the developers. This is the core set of roles needed to have a Scrum Team. Other members can include QA engineers, technical writers, database administrators, system administrators, user experience (UX) designers, interaction engineers, and anyone else, anyone who is important to creating the product. Part-time members are also allowed. They have to be involved in the commitment of the Sprint goal, as they are still on the team and no one but the team can commit to the goal.

Teams are typically made up of between five and nine members. A team can be smaller than five members, but really should not exceed nine or ten, the size at which team dynamics and communications tend to break down. If you need to scale, it is better to add more teams than to add more members to a given team.

It should also be noted that some people distinguish between the "Scrum Team," which includes the Scrum Master and the Product Owner, and the "Team," which does not.

The Scrum Master

The Scrum Master's role is to keep the team working at the highest level of productivity. The Scrum Master plans the iterations with the Scrum Team and the Product Owner. Further, she ensures Scrum Process is being followed and checks progress against expectations. She acts as a coach or facilitator for the team, helping the members solve problems, remove impediments to their progress, and learn to self-manage. She is responsible for facilitating the Review meeting and the Retrospective meeting.

The Scrum Master may be a developer on the team. Other companies prefer a dedicated Scrum Master, meaning the person does not program. A developer Scrum Master should not have responsibility beyond her team. A dedicated Scrum Master, on the other hand, can manage two to three teams, although with diminishing effectiveness as the number of teams grows.

The Product Owner

The Product Owner's mission is to represent the customer. He, therefore, manages the Product Backlog, in particular the prioritization of requirements. He must also be available to the team at all times to answer questions. Therefore it is best for the Product Owner to be co-located with the development team.

The Product Owner has the responsibility to make the Product Backlog visible within the organization, and it is important that this person takes input from his constituents and stakeholders. During the Planning meeting the Product Owner facilitates the goal setting for each Sprint. The team only takes direction or priorities from the Product Owner. People in the organization must respect this person's decisions, and if anyone wants priorities shifted, she has to go through the Product Owner. There are no end runs. Likewise, Product Ownership cannot be delegated to a group. The role must be occupied by an individual to prevent the team from receiving conflicting signals.

In commercial software development, the Product Owner is typically a product manager. Other titles found in this role are business analyst and technical product manager. For an in-house IT project, the Product Owner might actually be a department head or the actual end user.

Sprint Planning

Sprint planning involves two meetings. The first one is to decide what to build, and the second meeting is to determine how to build it.

What to Build?

The first meeting includes the Product Owner, the team, and may also include management, customers, and other stakeholders. The Product Owner leads the discussion by first reviewing the vision of the product and the progress made in the last Sprint. This provides the context and frames the upcoming iteration in relation to the big picture. Next the Product Owner discusses the priority of the requirements in the Product Backlog and what should be the included in the upcoming Sprint. This is the last opportunity to reorder the Product Backlog and influence which items make it into the pending Sprint. This is not, however, the time for a major debate about priorities. The Product Owner should have already socialized and gathered feedback on the priorities prior to the meeting. But if new information has emerged, this is the time to consider it and its impact on the next Sprint.

The Product Owner then facilitates the setting of the Sprint Goal, which anchors the team on the overall objective of the iteration and allows them to look beyond the individual requirements to see the whole. The Sprint Goal also gives the team some leeway in meeting their objectives. Documentation and anything else that needs to be delivered in order for the Sprint to be considered "done" is also defined in this meeting.

How to Build It?

The second planning meeting includes team members and any invited experts. The Scrum Master leads the discussion on how to turn the selected Product Backlog items into working software. The team then compiles a list of tasks to achieve this and meet the Sprint Goal.

Each task should be about four to sixteen hours of work. The task list is called the Sprint Backlog. Thus, a Product Backlog requirement might read, "Create an API layer to access purchase data," and a corresponding Sprint Backlog task might be to "map the purchase data elements to the database tables." Sometimes only a partial Sprint Backlog can be created, such as when an architecture must be designed. The team would reconvene at a later meeting to create the remaining task items when appropriate.

Further, the team owns the Sprint Backlog and only the team can change it. If, once the iteration begins, the team determines they have taken on more than can be handled within the Sprint, they will work with the Product Owner to reduce its scope. First, they will look at what can be removed from the iteration while still meeting the Sprint Goal. Failing that, they will work with the Product Owner to modify the Sprint Goal.

Daily Standup

The daily standup—or Daily Scrum, as it's called—is the fifteen-minute synchronization meeting for the team. During this meeting, each member states three things:

1. What she accomplished the previous day
2. What she will accomplish before the next meeting
3. Any obstacles that she is facing

All team members must attend this meeting, either in person or by phone. Email status updates are not acceptable. The meeting should always be in the same place, at the same time, and start on schedule even if all members are not present. Dial-ins should occur prior to the start of the meeting.

The purpose of this meeting is to keep the team members informed, let them know of obstacles that need to be resolved, promote quick decision-making, and avoid other meetings. The daily standup also helps to foster cooperation between team members. Non-team members can attend but are not allowed to speak and should stand or sit on the periphery.

Ideally, the room for this meeting has white boards, a speakerphone, and a door that can be closed to mute outside distractions. Chairs, however, are optional, which is why teams call it a "standup." If your team is courageous enough to do away with the chairs, you will find that your meetings will be more effective and end on time, because no one likes to be kept standing.

As each team member answers the three questions, the Scrum Master or another team member records the obstacles on the white board so it is visible and cannot be ignored. If the list keeps growing and items are not getting resolved, the team may not have the organizational support needed to succeed. In this case, the team may consider cancelling the Sprint, or calling for a Sprint Termination, which is covered in greater detail at the end of this chapter.

Feedback and the Role of Unit Testing

During the development phase of the Sprint, the team conducts the daily standup meeting, updates the Sprint Backlog in real-time, or at least once per day, and performs daily or frequent builds of the software. This all provides rapid feedback and visibility into the progress of the Sprint. In order to maintain this rapid feedback cycle and support frequent builds, Agile teams depend on unit testing.

Unit tests are low-level tests written by engineers to test the code. The purpose of these tests is to avoid the accumulation of defects in the code and to ensure that each iteration and new requirement does not break the system. Further, unit tests support refactoring, which is the process of rewriting the code without changing its behavior. This is usually done to improve its simplicity, flexibility, or performance.

Some teams practice test driven development (TDD), where the engineers write the unit tests prior to writing the code. This is similar to the way that a product manager might create an outline prior to writing a product requirement. Writing the tests in advance forces discipline around thinking through the problem and the boundary cases prior to coding, and also provides an explicit measure of when the code is "done." The acceptance test must also pass to be truly done.

Moreover, unit tests must run at a 100-percent pass rate and cannot be deferred. If there is a single broken test, the team fixes it before moving on to another Sprint Backlog task. Thus, unit testing differs from functional or acceptance testing, which is business- or customer-driven. With functional or acceptance testing, tests can fail and the Product Manager must make a judgment whether the software can be released with the known issue.

Sprint Review

The Sprint Review is an informational meeting at the end of the iteration for the team to present what was built during the Sprint. Attendees can include management, users, and customers, as well as other engineers. The Scrum Master or Product Owner typically start the meeting with an overview of the Sprint Goal and the progress against the goal. The meeting generally runs from two to four hours, and, because this is an informal meeting, the team should spend no more than two hours in preparation. Many teams even have a "no PowerPoint®" rule.

Unlike the daily standup, the Sprint Review is a working meeting. Observations, comments, and limited discussion are strongly encouraged, while heavy problem solving, if necessary, should be deferred to another meeting. In earlier versions of Scrum, especially for in-house development projects, the Product Owner, being a user or customer, was an attendee in this meeting rather than a presenter or facilitator. For commercial software, or in the case of projects where the Product Owner is a product manager, the Product Owner needs to be more deeply involved in the iteration and should know what was built prior to the review meeting. The Product Owner needs to use this time to ensure all participants understand what was built and whether priorities have shifted. The outcome of the review meeting guides the next Sprint Planning meeting.

Sprint Retrospective

After the Sprint Review meeting, the team takes part in the Sprint Retrospective. This is a one to three hour meeting to cover what went well during the last iteration and what could be improved. The Scrum Master acts as a facilitator in this discussion, guiding the team to inspect their process and make adjustments.

Again, the Product Owner traditionally did not attend this meeting because the Product Owner was an end user or customer. But in commercial software development, the interface between product management and development is critical to success and must be cultivated. The product manager should be given time within the meeting to review and brainstorm ways to work together more effectively with the development team. Scrum and Agile are about frequent inspection, adaptation, and continuous improvement, and product management needs a voice in this process and opportunities to improve it.

Sprint Termination

On rare occasions, a Sprint needs to be cancelled. This is called a Sprint Termination. Management may cancel a Sprint if the Sprint Goal becomes obsolete. This might be due to a strategic shift or the acquisition of a more mature, competing product.

The team also has the power to cancel the Sprint. This happens when: new information arises, such as the team learning that there is more work than had been anticipated and the team is not going to be able to achieve or modify the Sprint Goal; the team hits a roadblock that cannot be removed; or management meddles in the Sprint and tries to change priorities.

No one ever wants to terminate a Sprint. But it is the ultimate fallback if a team realizes it is unable to achieve a Sprint Goal for any reason. Except in the case of the actual project being cancelled, a Sprint Termination is followed by a new planning meeting and the setting of a new Sprint Goal.

We have discussed the basic mechanics of Scrum. With this foundation, we will extend the discussion in the next two chapters to Release Management and Release Planning from the product manager's perspective. Scrum will continue to be the methodology used to illustrate the principles.

3 Release Management

A release comprises one or multiple iterations. In the previous chapter, we discussed the details of a Scrum iteration, known as a Sprint. We are now going to look at how an iteration and release are managed, and in the next chapter examine how a release is planned. In getting to this stage, it is assumed that you have a product roadmap in place. The roadmap should communicate what you would like your product to do and when you would like it to do it. Further, the roadmap should be informed by your product strategy, which is in turn informed by your corporate strategy.

If you have not already done so, divide the roadmap into releases. Next, create the Product Backlog of the features that will define each release. After this, work with the development team to separate the upcoming (or current) release into a series of Sprints. From here, the development team creates the tasks needed to achieve the upcoming Sprint. The tasks are assembled in the Sprint Backlog and statuses are discussed daily at the standup meeting (Figure 3.1).

Sizing Requirements

Requirements in the Product Backlog are typically written as *user stories*, which are one- or two-sentence software requirements written in plain business language. The Product Backlog can therefore be viewed as a prioritized list of user stories. An example story for an e-commerce site might read:

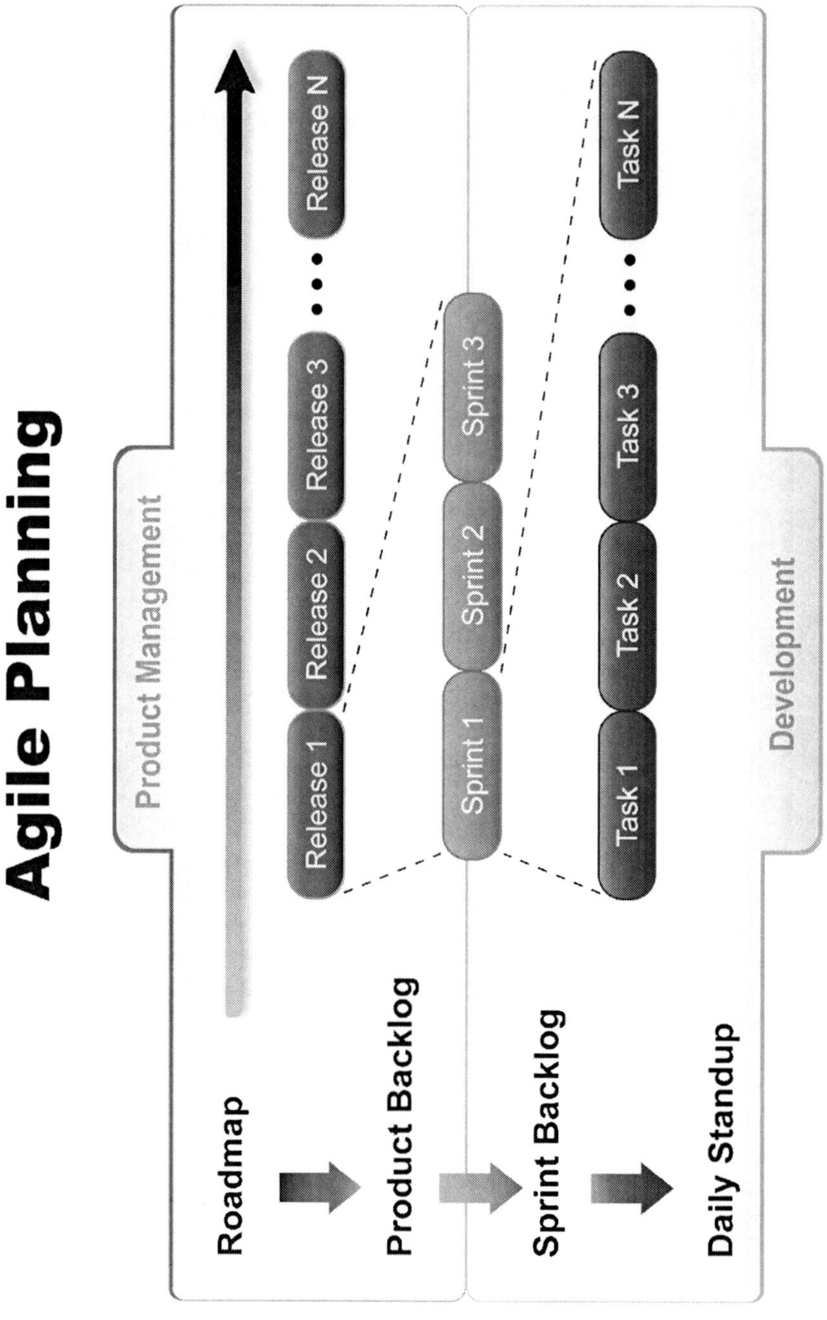

Agile Planning

Figure 3.1: Overview of an Agile release

As a merchandise manager, I want to be able to specify products to cross-sell at checkout so that average order size grows.

User stories are covered in detail in Chapter 5 on documentation. For now, I just want to introduce the concept so we can discuss how it relates to sizing a requirement and managing a release.

The development team estimates the size of each story in the Product Backlog. It is a rough estimate of the relative effort or complexity of each requirement. The usual metric is a story point, but I have used "truffle fish" and seen teams use "jellybeans." The reason for the fanciful units of measure is to make it clear that these are relative sizings rather than absolute sizings defined in hours or days. Thus, a feature estimated at 10 story points is expected to take twice as long as to develop as a feature estimated at 5 story points.

Occasionally, the development team will need to do research before it can size a story and understand its approach. In a situation like that you would create a research story, sometimes called a "spike." The research is given a time limit (in hours) and included as work to be done in the release, similar to other non-story work such as documentation. The actual implementation of the story will be pushed to the next or later release. Research could include exploring different technologies, prototyping, or testing some different implementations. Most importantly, the research is placed in the context of the other priorities; there is an explicit plan of action; and there is a time box around that plan.

Managing Velocity and Tracking Releases

With each of the stories given a size estimate, the team can now determine its velocity. Velocity is the amount of work the team can complete in one iteration. Velocity should be expressed in the same metric as requirements are sized. For our example, velocity would be measured in story points. At the end of each iteration, the velocity is calculated by counting the story points of the **completed** requirements (partially finished requirements or stories are not counted towards velocity). By doing this, we now know our throughput (*i.e.*, features per unit of time), which in Agile translates to how many story points of product backlog the team can develop per iteration. Velocity is then used to track the rate of progress and measure against plan, both of which we update after each iteration.

Tracking Velocity

By charting planned velocity versus actual velocity, we begin to see how we are doing against plan, and how even our throughput is measuring up from iteration to iteration. As the team gains experience, the members should become better at estimating. However, as long as they are consistent in how they estimate, the velocity measure will be self-correcting after the first iteration. Further, estimates for stories in the Product Backlog can be refined as more information becomes available (but estimates for stories being worked on should not be adjusted).

In the example below (Figure 3.2), we planned for the entire release, estimating the velocity for the project. As can be seen, we planned to start slow and then pick up speed. It usually takes a few iterations to reach a steady state. Although the team always strives to improve productivity through issues solved in the retrospective meetings, gains do become harder to come by over time.

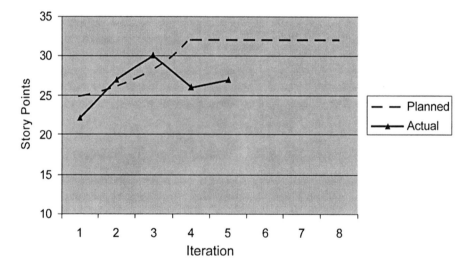

Figure 3.2: *Chart of actual vs. planned velocity by iteration*

After each iteration, you will want to adjust your plan based on the actual velocity of the iteration that was just completed. This example does not show how I would have re-estimated after each iteration. But, as you can see, when the project started our best guess was that we would level out at around 30 story points per iteration. The data, however, suggests the team trended to about 27 to 28 story points per iteration. Information like this is useful for planning the scope of future iterations, as well as for the release.

Cumulative Story Point View

The cumulative story point view provides another perspective that shows how you are doing against the release plan. Figure 3.3 uses the same data as Figure 3.2, but tracks total story points over time. The trend line shows our plan. You can see that we started behind plan, caught up by iteration three, and by iteration five were trending a little bit below plan again. If, in a situation like this, I am scheduled to release after the eighth iteration, I am going to start reducing scope and the expectations of the stakeholders.

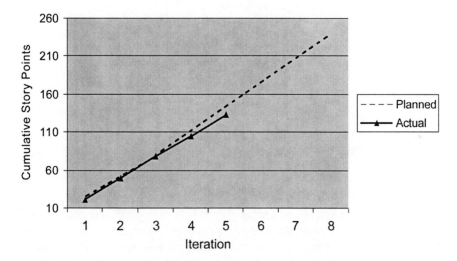

Figure 3.3: *Chart of actual vs. planned story points for the release showing work progressing slower than planned*

Release Burndown View

The release burndown (Figure 3.4) is the inverse of the cumulative view. Instead of counting up, we count down. Thus, it shows how many story points are needed to complete the release. At the end of each iteration you can quickly get a sense of your slope and how it compares to your target release date—you can even do this by tracking stories within an iteration (not shown here). For this reason, of the three views, I prefer this one. As can be seen in the example, although we are sticking close to our plan, it is clear that we are not on target to finish all the scheduled requirements by iteration eight. As above, I am going to start reducing scope and the expectations of the stakeholders.

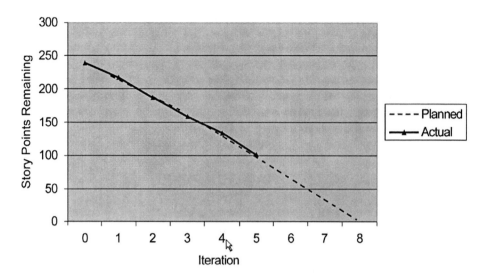

Figure 3.4: Release burndown chart showing work progressing slower than planned

Release Burndown with Scope Change

Scope change, also known as scope creep, has disrupted and plagued many software development projects. In Agile, however, we embrace change. As we go through the development process, we expect to uncover new requirements. If the additional scope being requested is higher priority than other features in the Product Backlog and necessary for the release, we support the addition as the right thing to do for the customer and the business.

Figure 3.5 illustrates an addition of scope. At the completion of iteration three, the team did not have negative productivity, as it might appear; rather, more new stories were added to the release than were completed. Because the team's velocity stayed constant, adding new stories put the team on a new trajectory. Agile makes the impact of scope change very transparent. As stated above, there are many good reasons to change the scope of a release. In this example, it has become clear that we are not going to be able to hit our release date at the end of iteration eight. We either need to change the release date or cut an equal amount of scope elsewhere.

This example also demonstrates another important difference between traditional software development and Agile. In traditional development, all scope change is disruptive. Even scope removal can create issues, because design work on all requirements is completed up front, and partial development might have already occurred. In Figure 3.5, removing scope from iterations six, seven, or eight involves no effort for the team, because no work has commenced on the stories being considered for those later iterations.

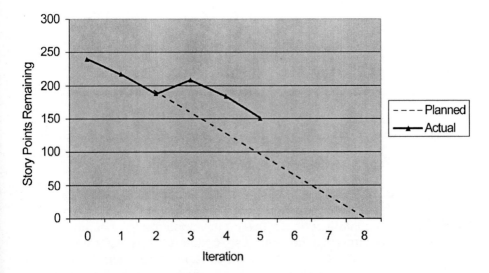

Figure 3.5: Release burndown with scope change

Managing an Iteration

In the previous section, we looked at managing a release using burndown and other charts. Maintaining these charts at the end of each iteration and adjusting the plan is an important task for the product manager or Scrum Product Owner. The development team uses similar methods to track their progress within an iteration, which can provide greater visibility into the progress of the team and any adjustments that might need to be made to the plan.

As discussed in Chapter 2, the development team takes the product backlog items selected for the upcoming iteration and converts it into a Sprint Backlog made up of the tasks needed to fulfill the requirement. Team members assign a time estimate (in hours) to each task and then update the number of hours remaining for each task. This should be done at least daily (Figure 3.6).

Task	Eng	Hours Remaining
Task 1	Raj	~~4~~ 0
Task 2	Peter	~~2~~ 4
Task n	Itje	8

Figure 3.6: Task board with task hours remaining

When the task is completed, the hours are set to zero. The team is not concerned with the hours spent on any given task, just the hours remaining. Thus, if two hours into a two-hour task, a developer determines he has four more hours to go, he will update the task to state four, as Peter has done in Figure 3.6 for Task 2. You can also see that Raj has completed Task 1, and that Itje has either just started or still needs to start the last task in the table.

Daily Iteration Burndown

The Scrum Master uses *the task hours remaining* estimates to produce a daily iteration burndown chart (Figure 3.7). In the example below, weekends and non-work days have been removed. As you can see, the iteration started off well. Then the team hit trouble in week two, and estimates on time remaining were revised upwards. The team then started making good forward progress again. Nevertheless, there is a big red flag. It does not look like the team is going to hit the August 17 date.

Because iterations use a fixed duration, we are going to have to work with the team to adjust the scope of the iteration and potentially even adjust the Sprint Goal. Figure 3.8 shows a scope reduction of about 20 percent of the original work plan on August 8. The team now has a new trend line and is likely to complete the remaining work within the iteration. The removed stories are placed back at the top of the Product Backlog and, thus, are likely to be the first ones scheduled for the next iteration. At this point, you will also be looking at how this scope reduction in the iteration is going to impact the release and whether any adjustments need to be made to the release.

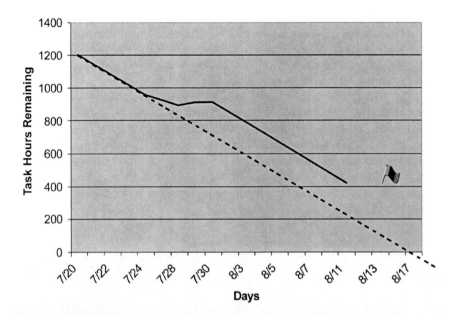

Figure 3.7: Iteration burndown chart showing a project behind schedule

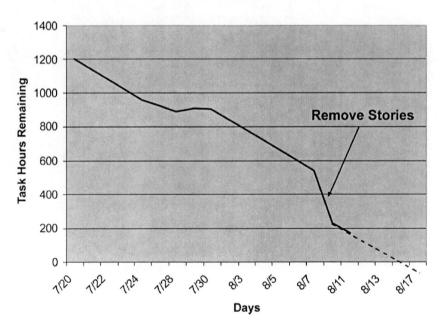

Figure 3.8: Iteration burndown with scope removed to hit the iteration end date

Tracking Progress with Task Boards

Your team will likely use a task board to track its progress. This will either be a physical task board or its software equivalent. Task boards are easy to maintain and provide excellent visibility into the team's progress on the iteration. Mike Cohn of Mountain Goat Software (http://www.mountaingoatsoftware.com) generously provided the image of the task board pictured in Figure 3.9. User stories and other requirements written on index cards are in the Product Backlog column (leftmost). The team turns the stories into tasks. As the task is worked on, it is moved to the In Process column and then to the Verify column. When the task has passed functional testing, it is moved to the Completed column (rightmost). You can also see the Scrum Master has used some open space in the center of the board to post the daily iteration burndown chart.

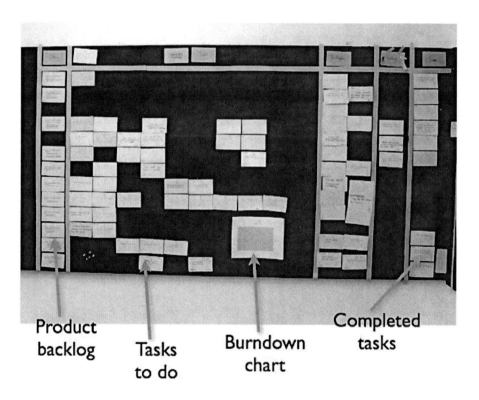

Figure 3.9: A real task board showing how requirements move from left to right as they are worked on in the iteration

To summarize, Agile makes it easy to know how the project is progressing with up-to-date information. The daily standup answers the quick status questions: What has each team member been working on? What will each be doing next? The task board visually shows where each story and task is in the queue. Lastly, the burndown charts track progress in relationship to time. As a product manager, you may want to attend the daily standup. The task board will let you know when requirements are ready for your review and acceptance testing. You will want to monitor the iteration burndown chart, because if the team is not tracking to plan, you will need to work with the team to cut scope and potentially adjust the Sprint Goal. If the team is ahead of plan, you might be able to add another story. After each iteration, you will update the release burndown chart and adjust the release plan accordingly.

4 Release Planning

Now that we have looked at some of the tools for managing a release, we will look at how to go about planning a release.

As touched upon earlier, planning starts with your company's business strategy (Figure 4.1). At most companies, this is provided by the executive team. You will then develop a product strategy that supports the corporate strategy and takes into account your market, your customer, the competitive landscape, and your technology. From the product strategy, you will develop your roadmap. A good goal is to have a roadmap that sets out a two- to five-year vision for the product. The roadmap should be reasonably detailed over the first nine to fifteen months. With this in place, and with a clear direction, you can begin to plan a release and the iterations that will be part of that release.

Create the Product Backlog

Using the roadmap, define releases if you have not already done this, and create the Product Backlog by listing the key features needed to realize nine to fifteen months of roadmap vision (Figure 4.2). The backlog should match the release schedule and be prioritized by business value.

Product Strategy in Place

*You need to know where you're going
before planning a release or iteration*

Figure 4.1: Release planning starts with a solid understanding of the business strategy.

At this stage, do not focus too much on getting everything right. It is an iterative process and the roadmap and the Product Backlog will change over time. You should, however, try to ensure that the requirements for the upcoming release are clearly defined. These will be the backlog items at the top of the list. Further down, the backlog items act as placeholders for work to still be done and to communicate intent to the team and other stakeholders.

Translate roadmap into releases and product backlog

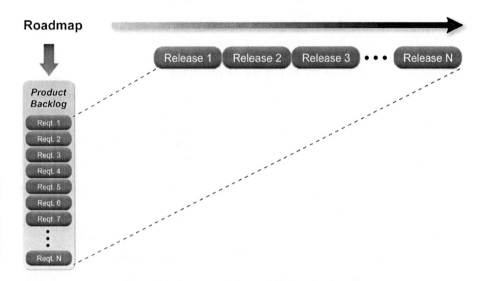

Figure 4.2: *Create items in the Product Backlog by translating features from each release for nine to fifteen months of roadmap.*

Map Sprints to the Release and Product Backlog

With the release and Product Backlog defined, we further subdivide it into Sprints. There are two approaches that can be used. The first is setting the release date and the other is setting the minimum marketable feature (MMF)[7] set.

---

7. Minimum marketable feature (MMF) is described by Mark Denne and Jane Cleland-Huang in *Software by Numbers: Low-Risk, High-Return Development* (New Jersey: Prentice Hall, 2003). The authors describe an MMF as a feature that "creates market value in one or more of the following ways: competitive differentiation, revenue generation, cost saving, brand projection, and enhanced loyalty." The authors further go on to state that "even this list is by no means exclusive, as true value can only be defined within the context of the proposed project and measured by the organization developing the software."

Fixed Release Date Planning

In fixed release date planning, we set the date for the release. We therefore also know how many iterations will fit in the release based on the team's iteration length. We then work backwards to see how much of the Product Backlog can be scheduled into each iteration. To do this, we use the team's velocity to estimate how many requirements or story points will fit into each Sprint (Figure 4.3).

Minimum Marketable Feature Set Planning

If the release date is flexible, determine the minimum marketable feature set and the total story points of effort to develop that feature set. Then calculate the number of Sprints required and the expected launch date based on the total number of story points that need to fit into the release. In the example below (Figure 4.4), we know we need to have requirements one through seven in the release, and the development team has estimated those at 60 story points of effort. If our team is averaging 15 story points per iteration, then we know that we will require four iterations.

Map sprints to release(s) using the team's velocity

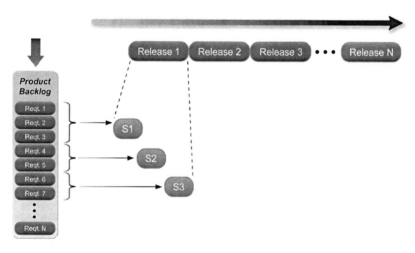

Figure 4.3: Slotting Product Backlog items into Sprints for a release

Minimum marketable feature set planning

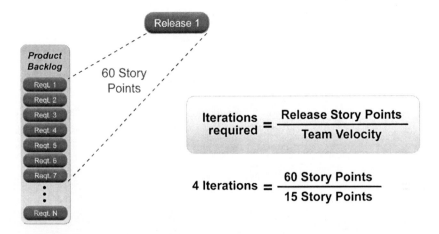

Figure 4.4: Planning a release with a minimum marketable feature set

Keep in mind that velocity gets less accurate when extrapolated over longer periods of time, such as six months to a year. It is still the best measure we have, so we will use it. But in this example, we may need to add, or at least plan for, a fifth iteration. It is highly probable the team will experience some challenges and that scope will expand beyond the existing four iterations and the 60 story points of effort as more is learned during the development.

Prussian Field Marshal Helmuth von Moltke[8] is famous for his assertion that "no plan of battle ever survives contact with the enemy." This is also true of Agile planning, where the enemy is the challenge of new product development. Although this is the plan, it only represents our best estimates based on the information we know at the time. We will need to re-prioritize and recalibrate the plan after each Sprint. Yet, as each iteration is completed, we will have better clarity and be able to plan with greater certainty.

---

8. http://en.wikipedia.org/wiki/Helmuth_von_Moltke_the_Elder

Iteration Planning Exercise

Life is never as neat as the idealized examples in books like these make it seem. In this example, you will be asked to plan the next iteration of the product. Each requirement is captured as a user story. A prioritized list of the stories in the Product Backlog with story point estimates is provided in Figure 4.5 below. Also, you need to know that the team completed 31 story points of development in the previous iteration.

STORY	POINTS
Story A	5
Story B	10
Story C	0.5
Story D	20
Story E	10
Story F	5
Story G	2
Story H	0.5
Story I	1

Figure 4.5: *Prioritized Product Backlog with size estimates*

Select the stories that will go into the next iteration. Please take a moment to go through this exercise before looking at the answer in the following section.

Iteration Planning Exercise Answer

Although this example was a little tricky, planning an iteration is still straightforward. We know the team completed 31 story points of development in the previous iteration. This becomes the new limit for how many story points we can put in the upcoming iteration. Because the Product Backlog is a prioritized list of requirements, we work from the top of the list selecting requirements until we have 31 story points of work. Requirements A, B, and C easily make the cut, and total 15.5 story points. Although we've only used half of our capacity, Story D at 20 points is too large to fit in the current iteration. We skip D and move down the list adding E and F for another 15 points. We now have 0.5 points of capacity remaining, so we look for our first really small feature, which is Story H. We now have 31 story points of effort defined for the iteration (Figure 4.6).

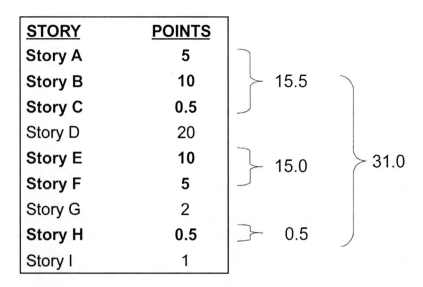

Figure 4.6: Selecting the highest priority stories for the iteration that do not exceed 31 points in total

If this were a real example, it would be a moment of truth for the product stakeholders. Given Story D's location as the fourth most important item, and its relatively large size, it is probably a much-anticipated feature. If this was the final iteration before the release, the stakeholders may not be comfortable deferring it. When faced with the reality of not getting Story D into the iteration—and thus into the release—people may actually decide to promote Story D and demote Story A or Story B. Another option would be to split Story D into two smaller stories, one to be completed now and embellishments to be added in a later release. Regardless, if it is decided that Story D must be in the iteration, Agile gives you the flexibility to make these trade-offs at a very late stage, when you have the most information available.

In addition to selecting the requirements to be included in the upcoming release, we would also set a Sprint Goal to provide a signpost for the most important aspects of the iteration. Within the iteration, the team develops in story order whenever possible. This way, if the scope of work were reduced during the iteration, the highest priority stories would still be completed.

Working Across Multiple Iterations

If you typically write big product requirement documents and focus on one release at a time, Agile will require some adjustment. For any given project, the Agile Product Manager works across past, present, and future iterations concurrently:

- Gathering feedback on recently released iterations

- Supporting the development team on the current iteration

- Fleshing out requirements by speaking with customers, testing concepts, and developing prototypes for upcoming iterations

Mapping this to the calendar, a good guideline is to focus on one hundred and twenty days of the product cycle (Figure 4.7). Assuming a thirty-day iteration cycle:

1. For Sprint T + 2, or sixty days out, gather feedback from customers about what the next features should be and how the product should behave. You might research a design goal, such as identifying obstacles that prevent prospects from converting to customers on your website. You should also socialize these requirements with development to capture their questions and concerns that need to be answered.

2. For Sprint T + 1, or thirty days out, validate designs, capture full acceptance criteria for each requirement, and complete each of the user stories so that they can be properly sized and developed.

3. For the current Sprint, support your development team by answering any questions that they have as they go through the development process.

4. For the Sprint that has just been released, validate the actual working software with customers to uncover any changes needed for future iterations.

Working across four or more iterations at a time-representing past, present, and future—can seem daunting. It requires a little more juggling in a job that already has too much task switching. But because you are working with smaller pieces of the puzzle at any one time and receiving solid feedback to guide your work, a rhythm is easily found.

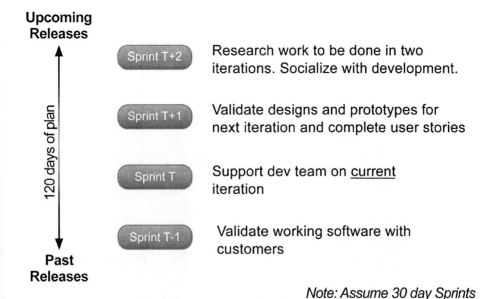

Figure 4.7: Product managers work concurrently across multiple iterations.

In the process of working across multiple iterations, you will be soliciting regular customer feedback on proposed designs and completed features. To support this, you need a large enough pool of customers to provide advice so as not to overburden any one customer with requests for feedback. Try to match customers with features that are of interest to them, or have customers who assist for a given iteration and then receive a break for six months or longer. If you currently have just a few select customers that advise you, look to grow the number by five to ten times.

Defining Requirements as Needed

In Agile, we deliver documentation as it is needed rather than developing it all up front. We therefore add detail as the probability of the requirement being built goes up. A detailed requirement waiting to be built can be viewed as inventory. Thus, the more time invested in that requirement, the larger your inventory or assets that are not creating immediate value. Further, we also want to reduce the chance that the requirement is going to get changed (*i.e.,* create rework) or entirely dropped (*i.e.,* create spoilage). By completing requirements at the last "responsible" moment, we minimize the risk of wasted effort and cost to the project.

Avoid defining too much upfront

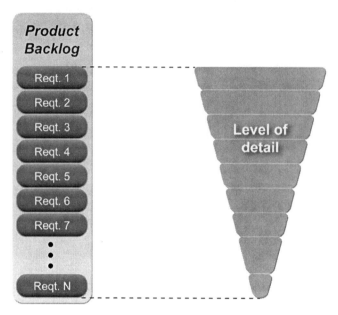

Figure 4.8: Detail is added to requirements as they move up the Product
Backlog and the probability that they will be built increases.

Agile's shorter lead times for requirements definition carries some risk that your
research will not be completed by the time the iteration starts. Therefore, it is a
good idea to have a few evergreen requirements. These are features that have
to be developed but are not currently urgent. Further, they are technically
difficult but require little or no input from the product management team (archi-
tectural changes, performance enhancements, and scalability improvements,
etc.) This way, if for any reason your research on a requirement becomes
delayed, you can at least slot an evergreen feature into the iteration and ensure
the team remains productive addressing high value items. Obviously, if you find
yourself frequently slotting evergreen requirements to fill capacity in iterations,
then you need to extend your research lead times.

The Role of User Experience Design in Agile

Thus far, we have talked a lot about the role of product management and development. It is worth noting, particularly in this chapter on planning, the importance of user experience (UX) design. Workflows, task analyses, prototyping,

usability, and personas are all extremely important in Agile development, as they are in any development. The difference is you need to get comfortable showing customers less polished work to help guide your next iteration.

Often, iteration zero is set aside for user experience research. Similar to the way we are now incrementally defining requirements, we do not look to answer all UX questions at this phase, just the highest priority ones. While this research is being conducted, the development team uses this iteration to set up the environment and prototype the architecture. Iteration zero is the only iteration where working software is not a deliverable.

Ideally, you are lucky enough to have dedicated UX experts. If you are using Scrum, the UX team can either be part of the Product Owner team working to define requirements (the ultimate decision-making authority still rests with the actual Product Owner), or embedded in the development team. If they are part of the Product Owner team, they are available to the development team to represent the user and answer questions, but they do not necessarily attend every daily standup. If they are part of the development team, the UX resource will own the first phase of the development process for stories that touch the graphical interface. The UX person will work on current stories that do not require significant user validation and look ahead to upcoming iterations for projects with longer lead times.

5 Documentation

One of the values in the Agile Manifesto is working software over comprehensive documentation. Documentation, however, is a major part of a product manager's role. If you are using a traditional development method, moving to Agile will change your approach to documentation, both in terms of how much you document and how you communicate via documents with your team.

User Stories

Many Scrum Teams have adopted the user story[9] for communicating requirements. These are frequently written on a physical index card, as pictured in Figure 5.1. The physical card is also the primary artifact for communication used in XP.

A user story is a high-level requirement that has just enough detail to allow developers to produce a rough estimate of its size. It should represent something between a half-day and two weeks of work. Stories longer than two weeks of work should be broken into smaller stories, and no story should be expected to take longer than the iteration. Large, loosely defined stories are known as epics. Epics can be included in the Product Backlog but need to be split into stories and further defined as they move towards the top of the Product Backlog.

---

9. Much of the discussion of user stories in this chapter is based on the work of Mike Cohn. Further information on user stories can be found in his book *User Stories Applied* and at his website http://www.mountaingoatsoftware.com.

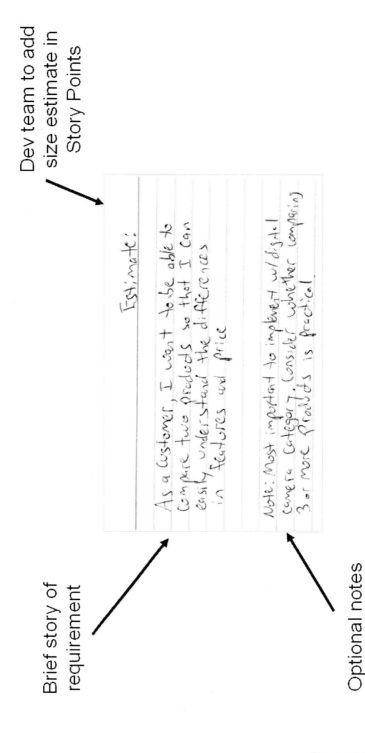

Dev team to add size estimate in Story Points

Brief story of requirement

Optional notes

Figure 5.1: *User stories are a popular format to document requirements and are frequently written on index cards.*

Chapter 5: Documentation

Most importantly, though, the story is a placeholder for a conversation between the product manager (or Product Owner, customer, or stakeholder) and the development team. Index cards are very effective because they force the Product Manager to be succinct and while not being so detailed as to replace the need for a rich conversation with the development team.

Figure 5.1 is an example for an e-commerce electronics site. The story reads:

> As a customer, I want to be able to compare two products so that I can easily understand the differences in features and price.

An optional note can be added at the bottom of the card with further detail. The note in the example above reads:

> Most important to implement with digital camera category. Consider whether adding 3 or more products is practical.

Reading into the story above, the product manager is indicating that the customer on the website would like the ability to compare products side by side. The note brings in additional design concerns. This feature is considered most valuable for the digital camera category. If it turns out that the comparison engine is easy to implement across the whole site, that is what should happen; but if it is going to take extra time, it should be implemented for digital cameras only. If, in the conversation, engineering believes it is best to implement it with just the digital camera category to minimize the development effort, this story would be split up into a comparison engine for the digital camera category and a series of lower priority stories for adding the feature to the other categories. Those lower priority stories would be placed further down in the Product Backlog.

The Product Manager is also indicating that the minimum requirement is to compare two products. This is probably the most asked for usage scenario. But she also wants some guidance around whether comparing three or more products is technically feasible and/or would work within the user interface (UI). These notes, like the story itself, are placeholders for the conversation, where the details would be worked out. Engineering might say comparing n products is just as easy as comparing two, at which point the Product Manager can do additional research, if it is needed, into how many products users really want to compare, and create UI mockups to see how many will reasonably fit on the screen.

All this discussion is done prior to the story being placed into an iteration. As the discussion progresses, the story is further refined until everyone has a clear understanding of the requirement. The team may document the additional details on the story card, in the acceptance criteria, or in an additional document, but not all conversations need to be documented. What matters most is that everyone understands the intent of the requirement. At this point, the development team adds its estimate for the effort to build it using story points or other similar metric. It is common for teams or subsets of teams to have separate pre-planning meetings to review upcoming backlog items.

User Story Structure

The user story covers three points:

- The user's role

- The goal the user is trying to achieve

- Why the user wants to achieve it

It takes the following form:

> **As a <user type> I want to <do something>**
> **so that I can <derive a benefit>.**

Looking back at the example in Figure 5.1, we can drop in the specifics:

> As a **customer**, I want to be able to **compare two products**
> so that I can **easily understand the differences in feature and price**.

User stories are an effective way to communicate requirements that tie into personas by specifying a role, and to express the desired capability and the justification for adding the capability. The story provides the context for the product designers and engineers to develop creative solutions to meet the user's need.

INVEST

Bill Wake in *Extreme Programming Explored* (2001) introduces six attributes of a good story that can easily be remembered with the acronym INVEST.

- **Independent**—Avoid dependencies between stories. Each story should stand alone so they can be re-prioritized in the Product Backlog at any time and not impact either the order or any other stories. You also want to keep the stories granular, so the highest priority elements of a feature get implemented first. This is also described as separating the feature from the embellishments.

- **Negotiable**—Stories are a starting point for a conversation with development. They are not a command. Many product managers have learned that the proper way to write requirements is to use the word "shall" to indicate unambiguously that the product must perform the described function. For example, "The customer SHALL be able to compare two products...." This works if you are not going to be speaking with the developers, but it is otherwise heavy-handed and likely to stifle creativity and inquiry. Take the time to talk through stories with your team and be open to alternatives that might work better and/or require less effort.

- **Valuable**—Always demonstrate why the story is worth implementing. If you are struggling to identify why the story is valuable, go back and spend more time investigating the story with your customers. You may have missed an important aspect of the story, or the story may not be worth the development effort and ongoing maintenance.

- **Estimable**—The story should be small enough and contain enough detail that the development team can estimate the effort. Epics should still be used as placeholders in the Product Backlog to capture important ideas and signal intent. But as the epic moves towards the top of the backlog, it will need to be split into stories so the team can estimate the work.

- **Small**—A story should represent between a half-day and two weeks of work and should definitely be small enough to fit into an iteration.

- **Testable**—Acceptance criteria for the story should be able to be tested to ensure the user's need has been met.

Acceptance Testing

Acceptance tests are written on the back of the user story card. The tests are used to let the developer know when the requirement has been met and to confirm that the product works from the user's perspective. A story is not complete and cannot be assigned to an iteration without acceptance criteria (see Figure 5.2).

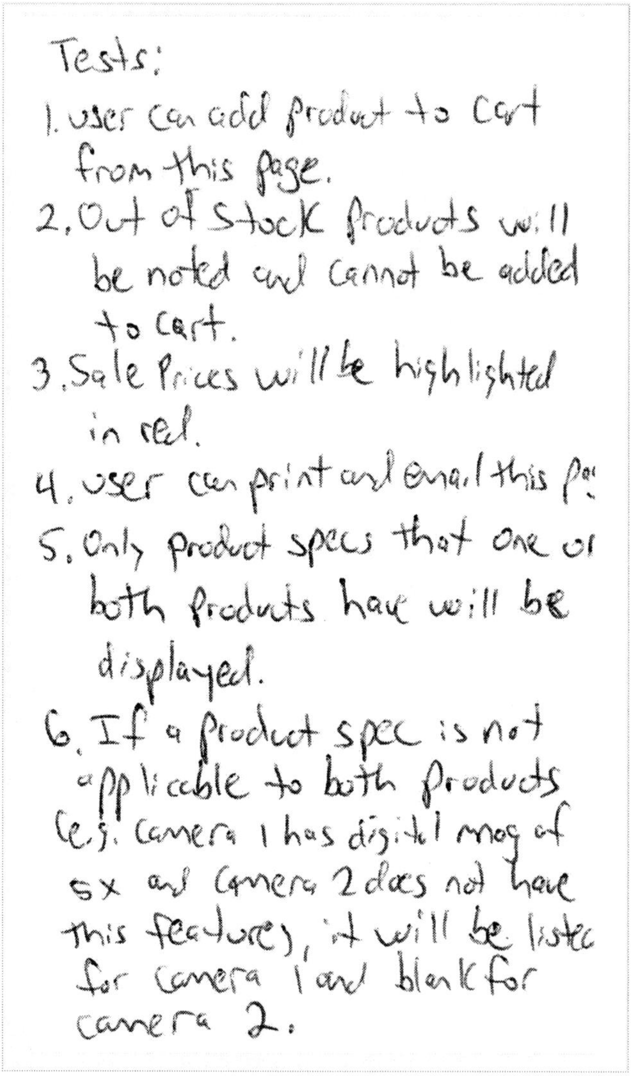

Tests:
1. user can add product to cart from this page.
2. Out of stock products will be noted and cannot be added to cart.
3. Sale Prices will be highlighted in red.
4. user can print and email this pa[ge]
5. Only product specs that one of both products have will be displayed.
6. If a product spec is not applicable to both products (e.g. camera 1 has digital mag of 5x and camera 2 does not have this feature), it will be listed for camera 1 and blank for camera 2.

Figure 5.2: Acceptance criteria are written on the back of the user story card that we first saw in Figure 5.1.

The acceptance tests for the user story example in Figure 5.1 read as follows:

1. User can add product to cart from this [*i.e.* the product comparison] page.
2. Out of stock products will be noted and cannot be added to cart.
3. Sales prices will be highlighted in red.
4. User can print and email this page.
5. Only product specs that one or both products have will be displayed.
6. If a product spec is not applicable to both products (*e.g.*, camera 1 has digital [magnification] of 5x, while camera 2 does not have this feature), it will be listed for camera 1 and blank for camera 2.

Acceptance testing is the responsibility of the whole team. As such, acceptance tests can be added at anytime by any team member. The product manager, however, should look to facilitate this process by sitting down with engineering and QA to brainstorm the acceptance criteria. As illustrated above, acceptance tests capture many of the functional elements and boundary cases of the feature. By communicating functionality via tests, it makes it easy to for the engineer to know when development on the feature is done and for QA to validate that the feature works. You may also hear these tests referred to as "satisfaction criteria." This refers to the high-level test cases that the feature should fulfill prior to the product manager, developer, and QA person brainstorming the full set of acceptance tests and boundary cases.

Acceptance testing is not a bug hunt in the traditional sense. The unit testing is in place to prevent bugs from accumulating in the code in the first place. Acceptance testing really focuses on whether the requirement was met. Other forms of testing such as stress or nonsensical input testing may also be warranted and would be conducted as an additional step.

Starting Out with Stories

If you are just starting out using user stories, start with high-level goals. For an e-commerce site that sells cameras, some high-level goals might include:

- The customer can search or browse for a camera that fits his or her lifestyle (*i.e.*, customers can find what they want).

- The customer can research cameras on the site, including specifications and reviews (*i.e.*, customers can learn more about products to guide their decisions).

- The customer can purchase the camera and accessories (*i.e.,* customers can find the whole solution at our site).

- The customer can save an order and return later to purchase (*i.e.,* customers can save their work).

Another great way to think about stories is to focus on the minimum marketable feature (MMF). What are the minimum capabilities of the feature that is both useful and usable by the user so that the product is potentially shippable at the end of the iteration? You can then use multiple separate stories for polishing the feature.

MMF stories are often bigger than standard user stories. For example, the minimum marketable feature for the e-commerce site might be:

> As a customer, I want to be able to create, edit, and cancel my orders so I do not have to contact customer support for assistance.

This story might also be split into three, one each for creating, editing, and deleting an order. But by keeping the story at the MMF level, prioritization and impact of scope removal are visible to all team members and stakeholders. Each team needs to decide for itself the optimal story size. But MMF stories are easier to communicate, and also ensure that the product could be deployed at the end of each iteration.

Non-Functional Requirements

User stories are best suited for functional requirements. Non-functional requirements typically seem forced when put into the user story format. A story to communicate that the product should run in multiple browsers would be written:

> As a customer, I'd like to be able to use the browser of my choice so I don't have to download a new browser.

It would just be clearer to write what is intended:

> The application shall run on Internet Explorer 7.x and higher, Firefox 3.x and higher, and Safari 4.x and higher.

Constraints and performance measurements can also be particularly challenging, because to be accepted they have to wait until the end of not just the iteration, but of the full release. In the example of multi-browser compatibility, all user interface requirements are dependent on this constraint.

Constraint Cards

Mike Cohn, in *User Stories Applied* (2004, 178–179) lists seven constraints with examples:

1. **Performance:** Ninety percent of product searches will return results in less than three seconds.
2. **Accuracy:** The software will dynamically generate and adjust reorder points to provide in stock levels of 98 percent for all standard products while maintaining less than fourteen days' inventory on hand for 95 percent of all standard products.
3. **Portability:** The software shall be designed to be ported to Android.
4. **Reusability:** The graphics rendering engine will be reusable by our other applications.
5. **Maintainability:** Automated unit tests must be written for all new code and be run after each build.
6. **Interoperability:** All documents shall be stored in XML.
7. **Capacity:** The data mart must be able to store one hundred and eighty million transactions (three million per month for five years) and support the real-time analytics tools.

Write constraints directly on the user story card and add the word "constraint" to the note (Figure 5.3).

> *The application shall run on Internet Explorer 7.x and higher, Firefox 3.x and higher, and Safari 4.x and higher*
>
> **Constraint**

Figure 5.3: Constraints should be called out and written directly on the card.

System Quality Cards[10]

Another technique for handling non-functional requirements is the system quality card. As functional requirements focus on "what the system will do," system qualities describe "how well the system will do it."

Below is a real-life example of a system quality requirement for a navigation system that was forced into the user story template.

> *As a Driver, I would like a faster load time for navigation, so I don't have to wait for it to load.*

In addition to sounding unnatural, the story is neither testable nor estimable. It just does not work well as a user story. Instead, a system quality card should be used (Figure 5.4).

A system quality card has six areas:

1. **Name:** The name of the quality (must be unique)
2. **Scale:** What will be measured, including the units of measure such as seconds
3. **Meter:** How the measurement will be conducted
4. **Target:** The desired level of performance
5. **Constraint:** The point at which the performance is unacceptable
6. **Benchmark:** The current level of performance

In the navigation system example, the engineers addressed the requirement across multiple iterations, using the first iteration to implement some quick fixes, including loading the navigation menu on start-up to later provide the user with a perception of a faster response time.

---

10. The discussion and example in this section come from Ryan Shriver, "Qualities, User Stories, and Sad State of Scrum Requirements," The Agile Engineer, blog comment posted October 12, 2008, http://tinyurl.com/ykokcrq theagileengineer.com/public/Home/Entries/2008/10/12_Qualities%2C_ User_Stories_and_sad_state_of_Scrum_requirements.html.

```
Name: Navigation System Start-Up Time
Scale: Elapsed seconds from when Driver clicks
Navigation icon until Navigation Main Menu appears
(assumes satellite connection is present and working)
Meter. Stopwatch timed from user interface
Target. < 20 seconds (performance of competing
product)
Fail: > 50 seconds
Benchmark: 50 seconds (Build 1703; Oct 7; First
start-up; Standard Environment)
```

Figure 5.4: System quality card for a navigation system

Splitting Stories

When stories are too large to fit into an iteration, or the remaining capacity in an iteration, it often makes sense to split the story into two or more smaller stories. This allows you to deliver the most valued functionality sooner and other enhancements later. In the iteration planning exercise in Chapter 4, there was a large requirement, Story D, which did not fit into the current iteration. Story D was the fourth highest priority story in the Product Backlog and estimated by the team at 20 story points in size. After the three higher priority stories were added to the iteration, there were only 15.5 story points of capacity remaining. The Product Owner was faced with two options:

a. place lower priority requirements into the current iteration and save Story D for the following iteration; or,

b. split Story D so that the most important parts of the requirement could be placed in the current iteration.

Using our e-commerce site example, let's say Story D looks like this:

As a merchandise manager, I want to cross-sell products at checkout so the average order size grows.

This story covers specifying products to cross-sell, setting the frequency that each product will be shown, setting an optional discount for each product, and reporting on the performance of the cross-sell campaign. It was also determined that only two products would be recommended to each customer at checkout for cross-selling and only products that were in stock would be displayed. In working with engineering, selecting cross-sell products and having the system display two at a time at checkout was thought to be straightforward, as long as it did not include the added logic of specifying percentages and discounts. Engineering also suggested that a data extract that could be opened in Microsoft Excel® would take less effort than developing a new report. The Product Owner, working with the merchandise manager, split and prioritized the story as follows,[11] and engineering added size estimates to the new stories:

> I want to be able to specify products for cross-sell at checkout, which the system automatically cycles through to increase average order size. (5 story points)

> I want a daily data file of the attach rate, dollar volume, and margin for each cross-sell product so I can optimize the suggested products. (3 story points)

> I want to be able to allocate the frequency that each cross-sell product is displayed at checkout so that I can test new products on a small set of customers. (3 story points)

> I want to be able to specify a discount on products suggested for cross-sell to maximize attach rate and profit. (3 story points)

> I want the daily data file to include seven and fourteen day moving averages so I can spot trends. (1 story point)

> I want to be able to specify a start and stop date for each product being cross sold so I do not have to make daily adjustments for seasonal items or products I am testing. (3 story points)

> I want a report showing me of the attach rate and dollar volume of each cross-sell product so I do not have to spend time importing it into Excel. (2 story points)

---

11. "As a merchandise manager" has intentionally been left off the seven stories to make it easier for the reader to focus on the differences between the stories.

With Story D now split into seven smaller stories, the first five stories—equaling 15 story points—can now fit into the upcoming iteration. This delivers the majority of the value to the merchandise manager without causing any additional delay. Furthermore, the team members now know the priority order of the five smaller stories that will make it into the iteration. If scope needs to be cut during the development, they know which stories to cut first and will still be able to preserve some capabilities that are of immediate use to the merchandise manager. It is also worth noting that the story was split along lines of useful value to the user, which is to be preferred when possible. Whether one, two, three, four, five, six, or all seven stories make it into the upcoming iteration, the capability delivered to the merchandise manager is functionally complete.

This example also demonstrates why splitting stories as they make their way to the top of the Product Backlog is so useful. There are three benefits to using more granular stories:

1. They make it easier for the team to accurately estimate the effort involved.
2. Iteration planning is improved because each story is less of the total iteration's capacity.
3. It becomes more straightforward to reduce scope (if needed) within an iteration without compromising the Sprint Goal.

There is a balance, however, for the product manager to maintain. Larger stories are easier to manage when working with stakeholders and planning a release. Smaller stories are preferred when working with development and planning an iteration.

Other Documents

Use of user stories is just one way to capture requirements in Agile development. But by no means is it the only way. Many teams succeed just fine by writing straightforward requirement statements and even producing more traditional requirements documents. Regardless of documentation format, the goal is to maximize conversation about each requirement within the team and have a workable method to prioritize, re-prioritize, and separate features into small enough increments to fit into iterations.

A product requirements document (PRD) is well suited for a complex product. The PRD forces the product manager to be disciplined in thinking through a feature. In Agile, the PRD may be more granular, with one written for each major feature rather than each release. Further, not every feature may merit a

PRD. PRDs are also useful in reinforcing the product vision to team. The PRD, however, will likely not be maintained under change control or tested against. It will be divided into story-sized increments and the stories will be used to develop and test against. Even if your company no longer produces PRDs, it is still worth reviewing the PRD template. You will still want to be able to answer the questions contained within, and you will capture some of these in the release plan (described in Chapter 6):

Product Requirements Template Issues

1. Project goals—tie project to product strategy with measurable goals, such as market share, revenue, customer satisfaction, productivity improvement, time to deployment, etc.

2. Timeline—target dates for key milestones.

3. Product Background and scope of release—describe whether this is a new product, next release, or an extension of an existing product, and if it will complement or replace any existing products.

4. User interface constraint—any standards to which the user interface must compl.y

5. Compatibility constraint—any external and internal interfaces and backwards compatibility that must be developed or maintained and may impact on other systems.

6. Scalability—system quality defining user, data volume, or transaction levels.

7. Usability and learnability—system quality definition for ease of use or ease of learning the system for a defined persona.

8. Performance—system quality defining performance goals.

9. Documentation—any documents that must be created, consumer of documents, and intended use.

10. Security—any security issues that must be accommodated and standards that must be observed.

11. Regulatory—any regulation that must be supported.

12. Manageability—any requirements for customer support, account management, or operations to manage the system and support customers.

13. Reporting—any new metrics that need to be captured and reported against.

14. International—any issues that must be accommodated to support international markets.

15. Assumptions—any assumption that could impact the project.

16. Open Issues—any unresolved issues that could impact the project.

The development team will need to decide whether to continue producing Functional or Technical Specifications. Teams sometimes use these to capture what was coded rather than as a precursor to development. Wikis are also popular for recording these types of details. It is worth pointing out that in XP, programmers document via the code, with remarks, and with the unit tests.

Lastly, establish standards, such as user interface guidelines, that define your company's approaches to software development. Because these details will not be added to each user story in the same way, they can easily be cut and pasted between PRDs.

Ultimately, each company needs to decide the right level and type of documentation needed based on product, culture, and regulatory environment. Recalling the Agile principle of "valuing working software over comprehensive documentation," all teams need to think hard about what documentation steps can be replaced by good communication. Also, are there any parts of the documentation that are not being used and can be eliminated?

6 Starting Out

You should now have a solid foundation in Agile development and a clear sense of how to work with an Agile development team. This chapter covers how to approach projects if you and your team are new to Agile. It also includes some tips and tricks for achieving success.

If your *entire* team is new to Agile, start with a small project. Identify a project that is independent of other projects and products and that can be handled by a single team (*i.e.*, fewer than nine developers). Ideally the project will be a new product or a from-scratch rewrite of an old one. Because unit tests need to be written, it is easiest to start with a new code base. If you use a legacy code base, it is not usually practical to backfill tests. Teams tend to add tests as they fix bugs or edit sections of the legacy code as part of adding new functionality. Therefore, it will be hard to build in the quality from the start and will take much longer to realize the associated productivity gain that comes from complete test coverage of the code.

If you are planning to showcase the team and Agile development within the company to spur further adoption, select a product that has an interface and can be visually demonstrated. An ETL (or extraction, transformation, and load) tool for data movement, for example, would not make a good candidate for a lighthouse project, because it would not demo well. Projects that have a frustrated customer and/or need to show fast results (*e.g.*, less than ninety days) are perfect choices, because Agile quickly demonstrates progress and value.

If your company prides itself on its audacity, you can also make an aggressive conversion to Agile. Salesforce.com, for example, rolled out Adaptive Development methodology in three months and then spent eighteen months in continuous improvement to achieve excellence. It was bold and painful, but the company proved it is doable. Salesforce.com's improved quarterly release schedule and customer satisfaction scores attest to their success.[12]

Selecting the Team

Stack the deck in your favor by choosing your first Agile team with care. Since everyone will be learning new ways of working, it is not the time to be working through team members' personal development issues. One contrary and difficult team member can spoil things. This is no different from traditional software development. But in traditional methods it is easier to avoid confrontation and isolate an uncooperative team member by shifting communications to email and documents. This does nothing to solve the underlying problem, but addressing the issue can be deferred without dragging the whole team down. In Agile, if someone is not meshing, it is obvious and out in the open. At some point, we all will probably have to deal with a challenging team member, but do not burden your first Agile team with this type of problem.

Further, pick team members who are comfortable making commitments and following through. In Scrum, the team commits to the iteration and what will be accomplished. The team is solely responsible for delivering against the commitment. Ideal team members take responsibility for their actions and those of the team and do not look to assign blame for any missed commitments.

Creating a Product Strategy

As stated earlier, you need to know where you are going to be successful, and product management sets the direction through the product strategy. If you or your team members have attended Scrum training, the term "product vision" might have been used. Vision is part of the strategy. I will use vision to mean the highest level of product strategy, which is the issue of the customer's pain and how the solution will evolve to solve it. Strategy will refer to the deeper thinking you need to put into the other aspects of your product. Also, it is important to continually reinforce the vision and strategy with your team, especially during the planning meeting and when setting the Sprint goal.

12. Susan Monroe, "The Year of Living Dangerously: A Product Manager's Guide to Surviving the Transition to Agile Development with Rasmus Mencke of Saleforce.com," *Silicon Valley Product Management Association News* 7, no. 5 (September/October 2008), http://www.svpma.org/newsarchives.html.

Continuing with our example of an e-commerce site that sells digital photography equipment, the company vision might be: "Helping digital photography enthusiasts fulfill their passion." The product vision, which might be considered the corporate mission (*i.e.*, how we will fulfill the corporate vision) might be: "The most comprehensive selection of equipment combined with the right advice to guide purchase for the digital photography enthusiast." This statement says a lot. First, we are going to carry a lot of products; second, we are targeting hobbyists; third, we will be providing advice that goes beyond the typical product catalog. As this translates into product trade-offs, we will emphasize making products easy to find and providing guidance to help customers find the right product for their skill levels and interests. This is very different from choosing to be the low cost leader, choosing to serve the professional photography market, or choosing to take a more paternalistic approach by carrying a limited set of "best in class" products.

The product strategy includes the necessary supporting detail for the vision to both prove its soundness and provide fuller guidance for design decisions. The product strategy includes:

1. The market problem and opportunity for the product, including:
   a. The target market and any specific segments served.
   b. The economic buyer.
   c. The user (The buyer and user may be the same person. In business software or children's software, however, the buyer is usually not the user, or else is one of many different users.).
2. Product or service description, including:
   a. The minimum marketable feature (MMF) set—Sometimes it is easier to think about this as the point at which the customer would choose to start using the product with all of its warts rather than wait for additional improvement. This is sometimes called the minimum viable product (MVP). Although MVP would be defined by your business objectives, I feel the word "viable" does not put us in the correct mindset to optimize the trade-offs between the desirability of the product and time to market, while the word "marketable" does.
   b. Competitive differentiation—Knowing the axis of differentiation is critical for prioritizing development. For example, a product that differentiates on ease of use will likely prioritize user experience design over adding new features.
3. Business model and ROI, including:
   a. How the company will make money.
   b. Expected return on investment for the project.

4. Positioning—There are the traditional four Ps: Product, Pricing, Promotion, and Place, and a fifth P for Proof points.

   a. Product—Product and differentiating features, as described in 2 above.

   b. Pricing—The product's price relative to value delivered, actual costs, and the costs of alternatives; the pricing increment of measure (per user, per transaction, *etc.*); the product's location along the value spectrum from bargain to premium.

   c. Promotion—How to move the buyer through the awareness, consideration, trial, and purchase cycle.

   d. Place—The channels through which the product will be sold (such as web direct, resellers, distributors, direct sales, retail, affiliates, *etc.*)

   e. Proof points—Evidence and examples that prove the product's positioning. This includes direct evidence as can be seen in the product, third party evidence such as customer references, testimonials, independent studies, and case studies, as well as competitive comparisons. Although it could be argued that proof points should be a subset of promotion, they are important enough to merit their own category and separate consideration in the product plan.

5. Timeline and budget—Covers what will be delivered when and for how much. The timeline comes in three levels of detail and scope. The long-term view is summarized in the product roadmap that shows how the product vision will be realized over time. The medium-term view is captured in the release plan, which is described below. The short-term view is detailed in the iteration plan.

The Release Plan

Once the product strategy is fleshed out, the next step is to create a release plan. The release plan as a defined tool was intentionally left out of Chapter 4 on release planning because the release plan is not an Agile tool and is not specific to Agile development. Creating a release plan is just good practice, and will make any product manager more successful. To produce a release plan, first put together a rough cut and then refine it as lower levels of details emerge through the additional planning and development activities. The plan should cover:

1. What's expected in the release and the theme for the release
2. Schedule of key milestones
3. Responsibilities and owners

4. Dependencies

5. Key messaging around the release

6. Risks and mitigations

7. Release goals

8. Success measures

Further, if the release is a major, marketable event, the plan would be expanded to a full-blown launch plan and involve a larger portion of the company.

Part of creating a release plan is, of course, selecting a release cycle. This depends on a lot of factors, including product type and complexity, the company's organization and culture, how quickly customers can absorb a new release (*e.g.,* does it require an install, or include big UI changes?), the company's capacity to support a new release, and the market potential for the product, especially in regard to the opportunity cost of delaying time to market. Other considerations include natural market rhythms[13] such as those found in consumer (*e.g.,* Christmas), tax, and school markets. Regulatory hurdles may favor larger, less frequent releases as well as the need for longer QA cycles. Even with unit testing, some products require a significant amount of functional and stress testing.[14] Guidewire, a business applications provider to the insurance industry, develops for eight monthly iterations and then spends the next four months testing. Further, it must be decided whether the release is date driven, meaning the product must release on a given date, or minimum marketable feature set driven, meaning the product will release when a defined set of features is developed.

From the marketing perspective, if you can do a Big Bang release and attract significant media attention, less frequent releases may make more sense. Certainly, hosted products lend themselves to more frequent releases. Nevertheless, it still may not make sense for the customers, especially if changes need to be communicated and training is required. Salesforce.com, for example, now releases four times per year since switching over to Agile. In 2006, by contrast, the company had a single release.

---

13. I was introduced to the term "market rhythm" by Luke Hohmann of Enthiosys, and prefer it to the terms "seasons" or "cycles."

14. Greg Cohen, "Embracing Agile Development," *Silicon Valley Product Management Association News* 7, no. 1 (January/February 2008), http://www.svpma.org/newsarchives.html.

Regardless of the release schedule you decide upon, revisit the decision annually and look to challenge the status quo. Your product is not creating any value until it is in the hands of your customer. Try to figure out how to deliver smaller increments of value to the market sooner. Keep in mind that if you have multiple teams working on different areas of the product, you can potentially release at a greater frequency than even your iteration cycle (eBay used to release every week, but their development cycle was longer). Determine the release cycle that is best for your customer and look to meet that target.

Creating the Product Backlog in a Hurry

Once the release plan is drafted, the next step is to create the Product Backlog. Ideally, the product strategy is in place and you know enough that you could create a product requirements document (PRD). You know your user, your market, and the pain your product will solve. In this case, it is relatively easy to start writing high-priority stories to get the process rolling. Just follow the process described in section 4.1 to create the Product Backlog.

Let's take a more extreme but realistic example. Pretend you are a product manager for a company whose management style would be best described as "reactive." You are thrown into an urgent project. The company needs the deal and cannot miss the already promised delivery date, which is less than ninety calendar days away, and, of course, neither you nor the development team were consulted on this date.

In such a case, you would call for an iteration zero. This gives development time to get their environment working and product management time to develop the highest priority user stories and validate UI prototypes. Remember iteration zero is not measured by working code. It is a time-boxed period to get ready to start building the product. If the development team, however, is already set to go, identify the first few goal stories that you know have to be addressed by the product and create enough Product Backlog for the first iteration.

A story-writing workshop can also help to get a project moving forward without delay. You can include customers, developers, and other stakeholders in this meeting. Start by gathering in a room and brainstorming stories. The stories can then be prioritized in or after the workshop to start the release. Make sure to elicit development for "evergreen" stories, which are the technically challenging requirements, such as architecture work that does not involve significant input or validation from product management and users. This will give you more time to get up to speed researching and documenting user-focused stories without squandering valuable development time.

Prioritizing the Product Backlog by Business Value

Once the Product Backlog is created, it is prioritized by business value. This is an extremely easy concept to grasp, but requires a lot of judgment to do well. Further, depending on the granularity of your backlog, value may only be realized after a collection of features is built. Therefore, you might need to group some of your backlog items for this analysis. You might also look to split a backlog item into the minimum marketable features and the embellishments.

Methods for Assigning Business Value

The preferred methods for determining business value are to (1) develop an ROI model for the product (*i.e.*, a product Profit and Loss or P&L), or (2) develop an ROI model for the business case of the customer who is using the product. For the former, you want to include time to market as a variable so you can trade off feature completeness versus revenue capture. For the latter, you want to understand how much money the customer will save or be able to make with the proposed capability.

As you move from new product to feature enhancements, assigning value with a strict ROI model can be truly challenging. Further, just because you can perform an ROI analysis in Excel does not mean that it is accurate. Most companies do not have rich enough data sets to know how delaying a feature will impact customer churn or new customer acquisition. If you are fortunate to be able to model this, by all means, use an ROI model method. But, more likely, value determination will be more subjective and become more so as the product matures.

Unlike the methods for absolute value determination, such as ROI models, relative value determination works effectively when the business case and cause and effect of adding or deferring the feature are hard to quantify. Companies, fortunately, have a significant amount of collective wisdom stored in their employees' brains. But there needs to be a way to tap it effectively, since each person has different influences and, without guidance, will come to different conclusions. Managers from sales, finance, marketing, operations, engineering, and client services, as well as members of the executive team, are probably not going to agree with all your Product Backlog rankings or even with each other, either. The product manager's role is to drive the team to agreement. There are a couple of techniques that product managers can use to build consensus around value determinations, and thus Product Backlog priority, when dealing with less quantitative value models.

The first method is to have a strong vision and place each requirement in the context of that vision. With this, you may be able to achieve consensus. Sometimes the choices are obvious. If that does not work, you need to follow a more structured process, using a tool called a prioritization matrix.

Prioritization Matrix

Creating a prioritization matrix is a simple five-step process. Include any stakeholders whose input is valuable to capture in this process. If the team is going through this exercise for the first time, allocate two to four hours to complete it.

Step 1. Place the requirements the company wants to prioritize in the left-hand column. In Figure 6.1, the requirements being evaluated are performance enhancements, single sign-on, integration with Salesforce.com, and support for the upcoming release of Internet Explorer.

Step 2. Develop criteria and place these in the gray bar towards the top of the chart. In the example below, the criteria are pain for users, percent of customers impacted, upsell revenue from existing customers, revenue from new customers, key product differentiator, and competitive necessity.

Step 3. Assign weights to each criterion. These are captured in the very top bar. In this example, 60 percent of the weighting is for current customer criteria (pain for users, percent of customers impacted, and upsell revenue) and 40 percent is weighted to new business criteria (new customer revenue, product differentiation, and competitive necessity). The example company is ultimately indicating that it strategically values customer retention more than new customer acquisition. If, after evaluating that statement, the management team determines that new customer acquisition is more important and that their current customers are not at risk, they would adjust the weightings. Completing this exercise is an iterative process that helps people reconcile and make explicit what they feel in their gut. This helps focus on the big picture.

Step 4. The team assigns values for each requirement. In this example, support for the upcoming release of Internet Explorer ranked highest with 60 points. The Vice President of Sales, who was representing the sales team in the creation of the matrix, might have thought Salesforce.com integration was the most important, but the matrix says otherwise. Because the Vice President of Sales helped create the matrix with the team, she understands that Internet Explorer support is a corporate priority that trumps the sales department's preference.

Step 5. Sanity—check the results. If the results feel wrong to the team, it usually means the team needs to do more tuning of the weightings or values. Maybe in everyone's gut, they thought Salesforce.com integration would be the highest priority feature. Maybe the team underweighted new customer acquisition, and therefore Internet Explorer support came out on top. Once again, by having discussions around the matrix's answers, the team recalibrates its priorities and becomes aligned. The prioritization exercise has turned the divergent, tacit knowledge of individuals into explicit convergent knowledge belonging to the whole team.

NOTE: The example here is a first-pass assessment at delivering business value. It does not take into account cost or effort. If you have good size estimates in the form of story points from engineering, add these as potential criteria. The criteria would need to be listed as "Low Cost" because you want a ranking of five to be the most desirable; in other words, a requirement that ranks five would be the least expensive to build. Now, since many of the requirements being ranked in this process are likely to be Epics, sizing probably does not yet exist. In this case, take the highest-ranking requirements from the prioritization matrix, develop the stories, and re-evaluate once the size estimates are available.

The prioritization matrix is lightweight, fast, and very effective. It is an easy tool to help stakeholders make their beliefs of value explicit. By focusing on ranking opportunities, it does not require advanced ROI models to be developed or guessed at. You can download a prioritization matrix template at http://www.agile-excellence.com.

Selecting an Iteration Length

The iteration length sets the rhythm for the team and the development. You want a cycle that's long enough to accomplish something worth demonstrating and short enough to be able to show frequent progress towards the goal and maximize feedback. I would recommend two weeks for a fast moving web service and thirty days for a "traditional" software product. Weekly iterations might be appropriate for an early stage product, or for delivering rapid fixes on a project that has a frustrated customer base and/or is in jeopardy of being cancelled. Likewise, iteration cycles longer than four weeks risk behaving like traditional software projects. Work with the development team to determine an iteration length that feels right and adjust it as the team becomes comfortable working in an Agile mode.

Prioritization Matrix

0 = low
5 = high

Application/Major Feature/Service	Overview	Requestor	Pain for User[2] (0 - 5)	% of customers impacted[3] (0 - 5)	Upsell revenue from existing customers[4] (0 - 5)	Revenue from new customers (0 - 5)	Key product differentiator (0 - 5)	Competitive necessity (0 - 5)	TOTAL SCORE
Weight[1]			25	20	15	15	15	10	**Total points** 100
1 Performance	Reduce screen rendering to < 2 second	Customers. Tech support	5	5	0	0	0	5	55
2 Single Sign-on	Allow our apps to no longer require multiple authentications	Customers	3	5	2	1	0	4	52
3 Integration with SF.com	Full data synch with SF .com database	Sales. Customers	4	2	0	2	4	0	46
4 Internet Explorer new release support	Full compatibility with upcoming release of internet explorer	Customers. Management	4	3	2	4	0	5	60
5									0
6									0

[1] Weight should total 100.
[2] Consider how difficult a feature is to use and how frequently that feature is used in assessing pain.
[3] Must take into account the % of customers impacted and their importance.
[4] You should count retaining customer who would otherwise leave as upsell revenue.

Figure 6.1: Filled-out prioritization matrix

Estimating Stories

As discussed earlier, the development team needs to be able to estimate the effort to build each user story. Sizing is a team effort and, if it is the team's first time using Agile, there are a couple of techniques to make the process easier. The first is for the team to rank the user stories by relative size (Figure 6.2). Then they take the smallest story and gauge if it is the smallest story the team is likely to encounter (*i.e.*, on the order of a half-day or full day of work). If it is, they set that to one story point. Then they estimate the other stories relative to the first story.

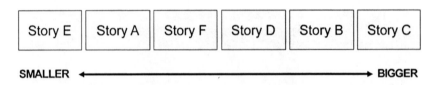

Figure 6.2: Place stories in order based on size.

The second method, first described by James Greening in 2002 and popularized by Mike Cohn of Mountain Goat Software, is called Planning Poker®. In Planning Poker, the team sits around a table and stories are shown to the team one at a time. Each team member picks a Planning Poker Card from his deck (Figure 6.3) and places it face down. Then everyone reveals his answer. The team members with the high and low estimates discuss why they think their estimate is accurate, and then the rest of the team shares their views. The hand is played again until consensus is reached. This method excels at encouraging deep discussion within the team.

The cards in the deck are a modified Fibonacci sequence (the next number is the sum of the previous two). This is to avoid a false sense of accuracy and encourage the team to split larger stories into smaller stories that can be better estimated. The zero card means the story has already been completed or represents just a few minutes of work. The question-mark card, which should be rarely played, is used when the team member is unable to make an estimate. If this card is used too often, the team needs to discuss the stories more and achieve better knowledge transfer within the team.

Figure 6.3: *Planning Poker deck[15]*

Testing and Beta Strategies

Agile presents opportunities to adjust your testing and beta programs to accelerate feedback and value delivery to the customer. For a Web 2.0 product with short release cycles, testing would generally be part of the iteration. For example, Six Apart, the creators of blogging software TypePad and Movable Type, releases every two weeks. Beta, in this scenario, might be an AB test on the site or an opt-in test. For client-installed software with long release cycles, you might add entire iterations devoted solely to testing in much the same way as Guidewire, a company mentioned earlier in this chapter, which releases annually and does eight month-long development Sprints followed by four month-long QA iterations. Devoting iterations solely to QA is more common when full scale functional, performance, and integration testing is needed.

---

15. Planning Poker decks are available through
http://store.mountaingoatsoftware.com/ for a less than a dollar per player (*i.e.*, estimator), or you can easily make your own if your company's purchasing policies make it too painful to buy anything that might make your team more productive.

Although the unit tests must run at 100 percent, product management still needs to address bugs that emerge from acceptance testing or that are identified in production. As a rule of thumb, bugs created within an iteration should be fixed in that iteration, and bugs found after an iteration should be prioritized and added to the Product Backlog. Sometimes it is appropriate to group a bunch of small bugs into a single story. Some teams, especially those moving to Agile and bringing with them a large bug database, prefer to keep a separate bug backlog. The product manager, though, still needs to prioritize and merge the two for a given iteration. I do not recommend keeping a separate bug backlog. It is just additional overhead, because most teams' resources are fixed and the bugs need to be prioritized against features.

Impact on Sales and Marketing

Up to this point, we have focused almost solely on the development side of Agile. Marketing and sales will also be impacted, as well as how product management interacts with these departments. This is particularly true if you can do away with or shorten your release cycle. In fact, you should be actively looking to deliver smaller increments of value to your customers more often. This will result in

- increased revenue, as a result of capturing more customers sooner;

- lower costs by not over-building the product (ultimately you will realize more value for less development effort);

- better resource and prioritization decisions due to faster feedback cycles.

As a result of more frequent releases, the marketing team will need to adjust its cadence. The team will be involved in smaller but more frequent efforts developing press releases, website updates, collateral changes, and sales portal updates. Because of shorter press cycles, the marketing team will also want to target new influencers like bloggers and online outlets where fast response is natural. The new metric becomes share of voice on a monthly basis rather than trying to land on the cover of a specific print publication. This model is more about developing a continual conversation about your product or company by always having something new about which to speak. This holds true for the press, the public, and customers. The goal is to stay top of mind.

ReturnPath Case Study

Matt Blumberg of ReturnPath has actually sought to apply Agile principles to marketing. ReturnPath's marketing department plans marketing projects on a six-week release schedule with two iterations per release and one or two themes per release. For each marketing iteration, the marketing team runs a planning session with key stakeholders and holds daily standups. Further, stakeholders can submit marketing projects to the backlog at any time. The marketing team also maintains enough slack for one or two opportunistic items that come up during the iteration. ReturnPath's experiment presents an early example of how an organization can employ Agile project management approaches beyond product development to ensure that the highest priority items are being addressed, visibility exists across the group and company, and collaboration and communication occurs between and within teams.[16]

Rules for Sharing Roadmaps

Whether, what, and how to share roadmaps is a favorite topic of product managers and Agile can positively change this as well. First, the sales team is a knowledgeable partner and product stakeholder. Treat them as such and collaborate with them through the requirements gathering, development, and launch process. With that stated, here are some guidelines for sharing roadmaps.

If your current rules for roadmap sharing are working well, then continue to use them. Develop external "blessed" roadmaps as needed. A big difference with Agile, though, is that the Product Backlog should be visible within the company, and therefore acts as a dashboard of medium term product intent (nine to fifteen months). Your constituents should know what you are planning in the current iteration (*i.e.,* what moved from the backlog into the current iteration) and your priorities based on the order of the items in the backlog.

Your team must recognize that priorities and roadmaps change and that a roadmap is not a promise. If a member of the sales team makes a customer commitment from internal documents, this is a training issue and should be addressed as such. You should not cut off the entire sales department because of it. With Agile this behavior is less likely. The sales team will have a much better knowledge of what is actually in a given release, as will you, because of the incremental delivery of working software. For companies with long sales cycles, being able to demo working features that are coming up in the next release can actually be a big advantage. Seeing is believing, and the prospect knows the sales representative is not making an empty promise.

---

16. http://onlyonce.blogs.com/onlyonce/2006/02/agile_marketing.html

With roadmaps and the Product Backlog, Agile provides product management with two great communication vehicles and the ability to be more transparent, get feedback on product plans earlier, and create greater alignment with constituents. I encourage you to leverage these and really consider sharing more detail with your customers as well. Open Source companies exploit transparency as a differentiator and a benefit. Even closed source companies, such as Chordiant Software, have placed transparency front and center with their customers. At the end of the day, transparency promotes better decision-making.

7 Organizing Around Agile

In this chapter, we will examine how to best organize around Agile based on project size and team structures. We will once again use Scrum as the example methodology. We will discuss situations in which the product manager is the Product Owner, as well as alternative staffing options. Although the product manager is often the logical choice to be the Product Owner, the role brings expanded responsibilities. You will:

1. Have to be available to the team to answer questions to help keep them at maximum productivity.

2. Need to write user stories or some other form of Agile-friendly requirement statements. Even if you do not change how you document requirements, the work will be more regular and steady.

3. Be more involved in writing acceptance tests, even if you have a QA team.

4. Either help QA do acceptance testing, or do the acceptance testing entirely yourself if you do not have a QA resource. The team should have automated unit tests in place, so in many ways the test burden goes down—but you will be doing acceptance testing throughout the iteration. Just like writing requirements, the work will be steadier.

Who Should Be Doing What?

Before discussing how companies have organized to successfully implement Scrum and Agile development, I want to emphasize that there are no right and wrong answers, just better and worse solutions. I have also discovered throughout my career that exceptions exist to every preconceived notion of how things "must be" to function successfully. I no longer speak to clients in absolutes, but rather try to share what has worked well for others and what has proved perilous. If there is any one lesson I have learned, it is that individual skill, personality, and temperament play a much larger role than title and reporting hierarchy. Therefore, one cannot say that product management should always be split between inbound and outbound responsibilities, or that strategy should sit on one side of that fence or the other. Rather, the answers are dependent on the product's complexity, the stage in the lifecycle, and the individual talents of the team members. Below are some guidelines on how you might organize. Do what feels right and track progress to determine whether changes are needed.

One Scrum Team

If you have a single, co-located Scrum Team, typically the product manager would be the Product Owner and retain full product management responsibilities. The product manager may own both inbound and outbound marketing. She should also look to sit with or next to her team if not already doing so.

Two Scrum Teams

With two Scrum Teams at the same location, usually product management and product marketing responsibilities will be split, with the product manager acting as the Product Owner dividing her time between the two teams, writing user stories and acceptance tests, and prioritizing backlog, *etc.* The product marketing manager will have the outbound responsibilities and work with all the other departments (*i.e.,* all departments except development) as well as analysts, media, and so on. He will also handle responsibilities such as pricing, collateral, and sales readiness. Dependent on the skill set, either the product manager or the product marketing manager will own the roadmap and strategy.

Three or More Scrum Teams

When you have three or more teams at the same location, inbound and outbound responsibilities are, once again, usually split. Often there will be one head product manager, sometimes known as the Chief Product Owner, who owns the strategy for the entire product. Each team will also have its own dedicated Product Owner, who might be a different product manager, a junior product manager or a business analyst.

An alternative model is to have the product manager as the Product Owner, but supported by other product managers who each own an area of the product. The Product Owner, who is probably one of the more senior product managers, owns the roadmap and prioritizes the backlog, while the supporting product managers support the team on their requirements, and as subject matter experts for their given features. In this model, all the product managers visit and work with customers, and need to coordinate so as not to overburden any single customer.

Distributed Teams

It is always more challenging to manage distributed teams. Regardless of development methodology, distributed teams will be less productive than co-located teams. Alignment and communication are harder because distance, time zones, language, and culture prevent a lot of the informal communication flows that occur when team members are located together. If you are embarking on significant new product development, think long and hard about whether you want to have a distributed team. If being distributed is a constraint that you must accommodate, Agile will give you better visibility so you can correct product issues more quickly.

Best practices for distributed teams:

- Each site conducts a local standup in their morning to address immediate issues.

- All teams join a daily teleconference standup, ideally scheduled at a common work time for all. A video-conference standup is better.

- Each location has a Scrum Master Proxy and a Product Owner Proxy. The proxies synch with their counterparts regularly and learn to guide their local teams and keep them productive.

- Team members visit other sites to deepen relationships and information exchange.

Technology can play a role in mitigating some of the challenges of distance. VOIP and webcams can go along way to overcoming cultural awkwardness and maintaining a co-located feel. It is worth the extra effort to get these technologies working. Distributed teams also need to implement a collaboration tool to function as a virtual task board. Examples include wikis at the low end and more specialized products like Rally Software, VersionOne, Xplanner.org, and Atlassian Jira with the GreenHopper plugin. There are many other tools, and you should be able to find a solution that fits your needs and budget. As an aside, if you have only one remote team member, the Scrum Master can usually support that person and the team can still even use a physical task board.

Managing Multiple Projects

Companies that develop multiple products with interdependencies need to ensure the product teams are able to leverage each other's gains, adapt to each other's changes, and remain synchronized. This is critical for companies that have applications groups, tools groups, platform groups, or just need to share resources, such as a QA group. In Scrum, communication across teams occurs through a Scrum of Scrums meeting.

The Scrum of Scrums

The Scrum of Scrums is a meeting of Scrum Masters (or other appropriate leads) from all the product and shared resource teams. Leads from teams not yet practicing Agile development still need to participate if an interdependency exists. Unlike the Daily Scrum that meets every day, the Scrum of Scrums is generally held between one and three times a week.

Mike Cohn of Mountain Goat Software suggests that the leads answer four questions during the meeting:

1. What has your team done since the last meeting?
2. What will your team do before the next meeting?
3. Are there any obstacles slowing your team down?
4. Are you about to place anything in another team's way?

Because this is a meeting of leaders, it is appropriate to reserve time to resolve issues after everyone provides their team's status.

Multiple Product Roadmaps

Companies that have interdependencies, and therefore need synchronization meetings such as the Scrum of Scrums, also need to consolidate roadmaps to communicate the timing and dependencies between releases. Product management owns the process of creating and maintaining the combined roadmap. The roadmap needs to clearly show the plan for each product and interdependencies. Figure 7.1 shows an example roadmap with tools, products, and platforms. Arrows mark the dependencies on the products and the platform. This roadmap is at the resolution of release, but with concurrent development, the roadmap may need to resolve to the iteration level.

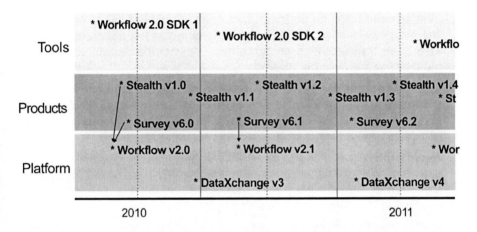

Figure 7.1: *Consolidated roadmap, showing interdependencies between the product and the platform*

Obstacles to Team Performance

Software development is always a team effort, and that is particularly true with Agile. When the team gels, it is a beautiful orchestration of cooperation and effort. When it does not, team members can become demoralized and, in the case of dysfunction, revert to unproductive patterns. Sometimes a team goes through the motions of Agile process but the results are subpar. Problems, however, cannot hide for long in Agile environments. Rapid iterations and information visibility brings it to the surface. Below are some of the signs, also known as *smells*, you can use to identify dysfunctional teams and obstacles to healthy team performance. Early identification and intervention are the best remedies.

Dysfunctions of Unhealthy Teams[17]

Patrick Lencioni describes the dysfunctions of a team in his book 'The Five Dysfunctions of Teams: A Leadership Fable.' The story focuses on an executive team for a fictitious hi-tech company but applies equally well to Agile teams. Lencioni's model has five elements that build on each other:

1. **Absence of trust**—An absence of trust between the team members is the most fundamental of the dysfunctions and that from which the others four stem. Trust does not exist when team members are reluctant to be vulnerable within the group. Team members need to be able to share openly their mistakes and weaknesses. When this does not happen, trust cannot be established.

2. **Fear of conflict**—Where there is no trust, a fear of conflict can emerge. Team members have guarded discussions instead of meaningful debate. This often masquerades as agreement, but honest debate and commitment to the plan will be missing.

3. **Lack of commitment**—Without meaningful debate, team members rarely commit to the decisions of the team. There is no buy-in. Each member reverts to focusing on her area of responsibility and will not support team objectives when they do not align with personal priorities.

4. **Avoidance of accountability**—With no commitment to a plan of action, team members avoid being accountable to each other and to team goals. Members do not challenge their teammates on actions that are counterproductive to achieving the team's objectives.

5. **Inattention to results**—Without accountability to each other, team members focus on their own personal goals, such as advancing their careers or the needs of their functional areas, at the expense of the common good of the team and team goals.

Although Agile process attempts to directly address these dysfunctions and does a remarkably good job at it, teams can still struggle to overcome them. Lencioni's model is useful for understanding the root causes of these negative behaviors.

If the team members do not trust each other, they will be afraid to open up and be vulnerable. Team members may appear to agree with one another, but there will be an absence of open discussion and honest debate. Other signs of this problem include team members changing the topic of discussion when the product manager, the Scrum Master, or another team member walks into the

---

17. This section weaves together ideas from three sources:

Patrick Lencioni, *The Five Dysfunction of a Team: A Leadership Fable* (New York: Jossey-Bass/John Wiley & Sons, 2002).

Mike Cohn, "Toward a Catalog of Scrum Smells," Scrum Alliance, October 2003, http://tinyurl.com/ycxjuqz.
mountaingoatsoftware.com/articles/11-toward-a-catalog-of-scrum-smells

Plamen R. Balkanski, "Team Dysfunctions and Scrum," Scrum Alliance, October 13, 2008, http://www.scrumalliance.org/articles/109-team-dysfunctions-and-scrum.

room. Another sign is a short Retrospective with little substantive discussion, especially if the Sprint Goal has been missed. The team might fear the conflict needed to resolve and candidly address the issues.

A second indicator is any member of the team blaming another member for a failure. The team commits to the Sprint Goal, and it is the team's collective responsibility to meet the goal. If an individual is underperforming and needs help, the team is expected to respond to assist that teammate. Blame is a sign that the members have not accepted their commitment and therefore their accountability for achieving the goal.

A third indicator is team members duplicating work, such as testing. When team members do not trust a teammate's approach and are unwilling to confront each other with their concerns, the team will push work underground where it is not visible. Work will not be mentioned in the daily standup and productivity will drop.

A fourth indicator is the Scrum Master assigning tasks. Agile teams are self-organizing and assigning tasks undermines the developers' responsibility to self-organize to achieve the Sprint Goal. If the Scrum Master has to assign tasks, the team suffers from a lack of commitment. Another issue regarding tasks is if a specialist is unwilling to perform general tasks. This individual is not committed to the team and its goals.

A fifth indicator is if team members skip the daily standup. The daily standup exists for the team to coordinate its activities and for team members to make commitments to their peers. It is an essential meeting and when run properly does not take more than fifteen minutes. When first moving to Agile, developers may consider the daily standup to be "evil management oversight" and even resist speaking. One remedy is to remove all observers from the daily standup until the team members are more comfortable sharing their status and discussing obstacles that stand in their way. If a team member still resists attending, and it is not because the meeting has lost focus, it usually means the individual is placing personal objectives above team goals. This team member will continue to require attention until he comes around.

Members of healthy teams with high trust willingly share information and offer help to each other. They are able to say, "I don't know." Team members in high-trust teams are also able to agree while disagreeing. Thus, they will state that although they do not agree with the decision, they accept it and will support it. As a product manager, you can assist in facilitating change by asking good, open-ended questions about approaches and plans, playing devil's advocate, and keeping the conversation focused on Sprint and customer goals. You cannot, however, ordain change. The team members need to want to change and trust each other before progress can be made. If the team has deeply rooted trust issues, there are steps that can be taken, and Lencioni offers advice in his book on how to build a foundation of trust. One example is to have team members share with the team what they view as their strengths and weaknesses. This level of change management and facilitation, however, is beyond the role of a product manager on an Agile team and will not be covered in this book. If it is something you need, it is time to bring in an outside facilitator and coach.

Dysfunctions of Healthy Teams

Not all issues are due to a lack of trust in the team. Sometimes teams willingly embrace Agile methods and commitment but still fall short. Ideally the team works through these issues in the Retrospective, but it is not always easy to see the problems that an outside observer would readily identify. Healthy teams can and do at times lose their rhythm. The telltale sign is consistently missing the Sprint Goal. Here are some areas where teams can get into trouble:[18]

1. **Customers provide little feedback from early iterations and then provide a lot of feedback on the earlier iterations when reviewing later iterations.** One reason for developing in small iterations is to accelerate learning. The product manager is responsible for ensuring the customer provides full and honest feedback. Emphasize the importance of the customer's opinion to the development of the solution. Regardless of involvement in the product, it helps to distance yourself from the product when speaking with customers so they do not feel that they might be criticizing you. You can do this by simply stating that engineering just finished this iteration and you would like to get their feedback on engineering's progress. Use phrases like "interesting" and "tell me more" to encourage the customer to continue to open up. Lastly, do not defend the design. Appearing defensive will shut down feedback. This is a time for listening.

2. **Stories are not being fully implemented in a single iteration.** It is easier to manage the Product Backlog when stories are larger, such as at the minimum marketable feature size. As the product matures, implementing new functionality often takes longer, as there are more parts of the system that are impacted. When stories no longer fit (or only just fit) into a single iteration, the stories need to be made more granular.

---

18. Amr Elssamadisy and Gregory Schalliol, *Recognizing and Responding to "Bad Smells" in Extreme Programming* (New York: ACM, 2002).

To minimize impact on Product Backlog management, wait until the last practical moment to split the story, such as just before the Sprint Planning meeting. Be open to further splitting in the planning session.

3. **A clean-up iteration is needed for the system to be production ready.** Teams sometimes feel compelled to maintain their velocity or prove the accuracy of their estimates. To do this, they might shortcut writing automated tests, documentation, or adherence to GUI standards. These are all necessary elements of each iteration and the iteration should not be considered finished without them; there is only one definition of "done." Do not let the team become a slave to its velocity. Velocity will change over time and the product manager's responsibility is to adjust the iteration and release plan accordingly and keep the team focused on the needs of the customer.

4. **Unit tests pass but the system is still broken.** If unit tests are passing for previous iterations but functional tests are not passing, it is time to start automating the functional tests as well. The extent of the test automation is a trade-off decision, but the better the coverage, the more reliable the system will be and the faster new iterations can be released.

5. **Large refactorings.** If the team is consistently consuming most or all of an iteration for refactoring, it usually means they have neglected performing smaller refactoring opportunities in the previous iterations. Speak with the team to see if they might refactor as they come across each opportunity and spread the burden more evenly across all iterations.

With new teams and teams struggling to adopt Agile thinking, it can also help to run a daily Retrospective (usually at the end of each day). This is the time to discuss the process, reinforce good habits, and ask the types of questions you expect the team to be asking itself once up to speed. Over time, the daily Retrospective can be dropped for the single Retrospective at the end of the iteration.

Staffing Teams

As software development evolves, so do the skills required of technical staff to succeed. Engineers used to be hired based on technical competence; there were problems to be solved and businesses needed experts to solve them. Then businesses realized that it was not enough to only be technically competent. Engineers also needed to have good communication skills. This was necessary to work effectively with peers and management. Agile now places a third demand on engineers: they must be good team players. Not all engineers, however, enjoy being part of a team. Even fewer are comfortable with practices such as pair programming.

To the extent that it is in your control or sphere of influence, it is important to distinguish between the able (good team players), the willing (not currently good team players but have the desire to learn), and the unwilling (not good team players and lacking all desire to change). It benefits no one to put a maverick or a prima donna on the team. The individual will be unhappy, as will the rest of the team. Engineers and other employees who are not team players and not interested in acquiring the skills should be moved to individual contributor roles within the company. If individual contributor roles are not available or do not exist, it is best to work with that person to find a new opportunity at another company that matches the individual's skill set and temperament. This is truly the only responsible course of action.

The Agile engineer is technically competent (brilliant is better), a good communicator, and a willing team player. Look for these three characteristics when hiring and staffing a team. If someone is not fitting in and is not likely to change, provide an opportunity for a graceful exit. Everyone will be happier and better off for it.

8 A Look at Extreme Programming and Lean Software Development

In our search for agility, we need to understand what will work best for our companies and products. It is, therefore, helpful to understand different flavors of Agile. We have mostly focused on Scrum up to this point, and, with that grounding, we will now look at two other methodologies: Extreme Programming (XP) and Lean Software Development.

Extreme Programming

Kent Beck, the father of XP, developed this technique in 1996 while working on a payroll system at Chrysler. He published his lessons in 2000 in the book 'Extreme Programming Explained.' He writes, "XP is a lightweight methodology for small-to-medium-sized teams developing software in the face of vague or rapidly changing requirements."[19]

Beck's goal was to deliver value quickly, so some of the key words here are:

1. "lightweight"
2. "small to medium teams"
3. "vague or rapidly changing requirements"

---

19. Beck, *Extreme Programming Explained*, xv.

First, what makes XP so Extreme? XP takes common sense development principles to an extreme level. If code reviews are considered good practice, perform continual code review by programming in pairs. If testing helps produce bug-free code, write automated unit tests that run multiple times during the day and perform frequent end user and functional tests. If refactoring helps improve code, developers should always look for opportunities to do it. If integration testing helps uncover issues, complete software builds once or multiple times a day.

XP, like other Agile methods, focuses on short iterations. Instead of designing the whole system, building the whole system, and testing the whole system, an XP team works to design, build, and test a thin functional slice of the system that works end to end. XP also values simplicity. It focuses on delivering the simplest design to support the current functionality and nothing more.

XP's Core Values

XP has four core values:

1. **Communication**—Practices are deliberately set up to ensure communication between developers and business users, including the practices of estimating, pair programming, and acceptance testing.

2. **Simplicity**—It is better to meet only the current need today and pay a little more tomorrow to change it if the requirement grows than to place a bet by developing more complicated functionality that may never be used. Basically, hedging in software development is not profitable. To step outside of XP for a moment and view the issue from a Lean development perspective, writing code that is not going to be used immediately is like carrying perishable inventory: it may spoil before it is ever needed.

3. **Feedback**—Feedback is everywhere in XP. Automated unit tests run multiple times a day; the product manager (or business user) receives size estimates on the stories that let her know if the requirement is clear and practical to implement; velocity is tracked against plan, product managers and customers do acceptance testing; and the system is used in production sooner rather than later. These all provide opportunities for rapid and meaningful feedback.

4. **Courage**—Developers need the courage to move fast, to throw out and refactor code, to try new approaches, and to play to win. Rather than trying to shield yourself from blame, also known as *covering your back* (or the more colorful CYA) have the courage to always be reaching to deliver the most value to the customer.

XP's Core Practices

XP also has twelve core practices:

1. **The planning game**—Determines the scope of next release by balancing business priorities and technical estimates. The product manager decides the priorities and balances scope and dates while development owns estimates, process, technical consequences, and detailed scheduling of the development.

2. **Small releases**—Place a simple system into production early and lower risk by planning and delivering in small increments.

3. **Metaphor**—XP's name for architecture. The system metaphor uses a shared story and vocabulary of how the system works that is understood by business and technical team members to guide development.

4. **Simple design**—Keep the design as simple as possible and avoid adding anything that is not needed to support the current functionality. As the system develops, remove complexity when it is found.

5. **Testing**—Developers write unit tests that must run at 100 percent before development can continue, and the Product Manager (or customer or QA) writes functional tests to confirm the requirement is met.

6. **Refactoring**—Without changing its behavior, developers find opportunities to restructure the system to simplify, add flexibility, and improve performance. This is only possible because of the focus on unit testing.

7. **Pair programming**—Two developers work at one machine, alternating who is programming and who is reviewing.

8. **Collective ownership**—Any developer can change any code anywhere at anytime.

9. **Continuous improvement**—Every time a development task is completed, the system goes through integration and build, which usually occurs multiple times a day.

10. **Forty-hour week**—Developers should work only forty hours a week and never put in overtime two weeks in a row. In general Agile speak, this rule is often called "sustainable pace," the thought being that a developer needs to be well rested to write effective code. If he is working 60–80 hours a week, the code will suffer, his personal life will bleed into his work life, with shopping, email, reading news, *etc.* It is better to arrive at the office, work a full day, go home to relax, and then come in refreshed the next morning.

11. **On-site customer**—XP advocates a real user, on-site and on the team to answer questions at all times. In commercial software development, this on-site customer can be a product manager or the equivalent of the Scrum Product Owner.

12. **Coding standards**—All code will be written to standards that highlight communication through the code so that the team members can move around easily and work on another member's code.

I agree with all the XP practices, especially the forty-hour week. Further, teams will only realize the full benefits of XP by following all twelve practices. There are three practices—the Planning Game, testing, and continuous integration—that touch at the heart of product management and merit further exploration.

The Planning Game defines the interaction and responsibilities of those representing business interests (*i.e.,* product management) and technical interests (*i.e.,* development.) It fosters a healthy and honest dialogue around the requirements, implications, and optimal business solution that is also feasible. In XP, requirements are written down on story cards and act as placeholders for conversations. The two-way conversation over a story is inevitably more productive than the one-way conversation that tends to happen during a product requirements review. The audience does not nod off in a story review because it is chunked small enough, and the conversation is interactive enough to remain interesting. If the product has complex business logic that needs to be conveyed, a supplemental document can be added to the story. However, using stories and conversation remains a more natural way to communicate business needs if your aim is to develop, and receive feedback on, the technical implications of the request.

Development then uses relative measures, such as story points, to estimate size and effort. This ends up being very effective at providing a true picture of throughput or velocity of the team, which is a key input for the release and iteration planning. As we saw in Chapter 4 on release planning, once the team's velocity is known, planning is simple. Take the prioritized stack of story cards and count out as many story points as the team can accommodate based on its past velocity. The product manager can make realistic assessments of what will be in the next iterations and when a release will be ready, or whether scope needs to be trimmed to hit a date. XP planning requires little overhead and proves to be much more objective than traditional software release planning. I have observed with traditional software development that pleading with the development manager can actually open up capacity in a release without impacting any of the *planned* dates. The actual release dates, however, have been known to vary in unpredictable ways. XP prevents people being told what they want to hear regarding scope and release dates. It supports informed decision-making and trade-offs.

The automated unit testing that the team builds as each new feature is developed results in solid code. This eliminates significant risk of late changes that the team may have to make due to design decisions (*e.g.,* performance) or clarification around a requirement. Further, bug fixes tend not to introduce new bugs, and fixed bugs do not reappear because a new test is written for every bug that is found. Without unit tests, when an urgent patch was needed on a product already in production, I would work with the developer to attempt to assess the risk of the fix breaking another area of the program. Although this kind of inquiry is still warranted, with unit testing, you know with a high-level of confidence and some absolute measure of certainty that the fix has not changed the behavior in another part of the system.

Lastly, in addition to contributing to the quality of the system, continuous integration provides the product manager with visibility into the progress of the development effort. Being able to see working code allows her to confirm early in the process that requirements were correctly communicated and understood. By catching communication gaps early, they can be corrected with little impact to schedule and the quality of the product.

Tasks and XP

XP teams tend not to break stories down into tasks. The burndown chart is based on story points or stories remaining. The reason for this is simple: XP practitioners believe that the planning meeting, which occurs at the beginning of the iteration, is the point at which the team knows the least about the implementation. Thus, to create and commit to tasks would be ill-advised. Better to give the developer the freedom to optimize the implementation once she has reviewed the requirement, the code, and its implications. Skipping the creation and estimating of tasks also has the benefit of requiring less planning and estimating time from the development team.

Lean Software Development

Lean Software Development ("Lean") applies the Lean manufacturing philosophies developed by Toyota (a.k.a. Toyota Production System) to software development. Its main focus is on the flow of value through the development process by the frequent delivery of useful increments of working software. This is achieved by focusing the team on leveling (maintaining steady work through each phase of the development cycle), minimizing the overall work in progress (WIP), and reducing cycle time.

Mary and Tom Poppendieck adapted the manufacturing methods to software development and published them in their 2003 book entitled 'Lean Software Development.' They elaborated upon seven key principles of Lean:

1. Eliminate waste
2. Build integrity in
3. See the whole
4. Decide as late as possible
5. Deliver as fast as possible
6. Amplify learning
7. Empower the team

Below, I will discuss these principles in various depths as they relate to product management and to the extent that they go beyond the Agile concepts already covered. For a full treatment of the topic, consult the Poppendiecks' book.[20]

Eliminate Waste

"Eliminate waste" is the most fundamental of the seven principles. Waste is defined as anything that does not create value for the customer. Within this principle, Toyota has defined seven types of manufacturing waste. Mary and Tom Poppendieck adjusted those to describe seven categories of software development waste:

1. **Partially done work**—Anything in the software development process that is not finished and released to the customer is considered unfinished. Thus, requirements that have yet to be built, completed code that has not been integrated into the system, code waiting to be tested, and code waiting to be deployed are all partially done work. Lean looks to minimize work in any of these states.
2. **Extra processes**—Unnecessary paperwork and sign-offs are probably the biggest waste in this category. For each process, figure out if there is a recipient and what is the minimum that is needed.

---

20. Mary Poppendieck and Tom Poppendieck, *Lean Software Development: An Agile Toolkit* (Indianapolis: Addison-Wesley Professional, 2003).

3. **Extra features**—Extra features include obvious things like unused capabilities. But the category also includes code that is expected to be leveraged in the future but is not currently being used. All code has to be maintained and carries a cost. If it is not needed, just like in XP, leave it out of the product.

4. **Task switching**—It takes time to switch tasks. It is, therefore, most efficient to let your developers focus on one task and one project at a time. Any more than this will create waste.

5. **Waiting**—Any delays that keep a customer from realizing value is waste. Further, if the customer cannot realize value, your company cannot realize value either. Lean looks to minimize waste in everything from approvals and requirements to coding, testing, *etc.*

6. **Motion**—Motion is considered wasteful. Work to minimize motion and effort for developers to get questions answered and to know the status of tests. This also applies to the motion of documents and artifacts. Every time a document moves from one person to the next, such as a product manager to a designer, there is an opportunity for misinterpretation and waste.

7. **Defects**—This gets a little complicated, but the cost of a defect is the product of the impact of the defect and the time it takes to detect it (*i.e.,* impact multiplied by time). So a major defect that is found in minutes during development produces little waste. A small defect, however, that lingers for weeks in production can produce much greater waste, as a lot of effort needs to go into logging the issue, communicating it to the correct employees, understanding the cause, correcting it, testing the fix, and deploying it into production. Small defects found in production often require an outsized effort to fix.

One tool to identify waste is Value Stream mapping. Creating a first pass Value Stream should be kept at a high-level and not take your team more than an hour or two. First, map the major steps in a process and the time it takes to perform each step. This is known as "work time" or "value added time." Then map the wait time or non-value added time that is spent between each step. By comparing the work time to the total time for the process, the process cycle efficiency can be calculated.

The Value Stream in Figure 8.1 was based on a traditional development project on which I worked. The Process Cycle efficiency was 41 percent. Basically, out of a 290-day process, we only added value for 120 days of that time. Now, looking at the hand-offs, the team was actually reasonably efficient, but then **boom!**—there was a giant queue for migrating customers that averaged 150 days and, truth be told, the last customer to be migrated switched nine months after the product was deployed to production. More amazing still, this was for a release that all the customers considered highly important. So, for this process, it would be easy to accelerate value delivery by improving migration times.

The Value Stream map in Figure 8.2 provides a nice contrast to the previous map. This is a map for the most efficient Agile project on which I have worked. There is minimal non-value add time. Admittedly, it is not fair to try to draw perfect parallels between the two Value Streams. They were for very different types of product. You can, however, see that in the 290 days it took to deliver the product in Figure 8.1, the team would have completed thirteen iterations on the second project and would likely have been able to deliver more to the customer in the same period of time and even deliver it sooner.

Value Stream mapping can help uncover constraints in your processes, and you can get a big boost if you can remove those constraints. Also, if you are performing a non-value adding activity (*i.e.*, one with no audience for the output, but which you may have to do as a contractual obligation) spend the minimum possible time on it. Often, non-value added time can be found in wait times for approvals, to get a project into QA, or for documentation. Value Stream maps can shed light on these areas and help make your company more efficient.

If the high-level mapping proves useful, it can be followed up with an in-depth Value Stream Map analysis. This usually takes closer to three days and includes mapping the current state, envisioning the future state, and creating an implementation plan. Expect the actual implementation of the future state plan to take anywhere from a month to a year depending on the level of change required.[21]

Build Integrity In

Product integrity deals with how well a product meets the customer's objectives and how well it "fits together." It thus has an external and internal component. The Poppendiecks label these *perceived integrity* and *conceptual integrity*, respectively.

---

21. Drew A. Locher, *Value Stream Mapping for Lean Development: A How to Guide for Streamlining Time to Market* (New York: CRC Press, 2008), 1–2.

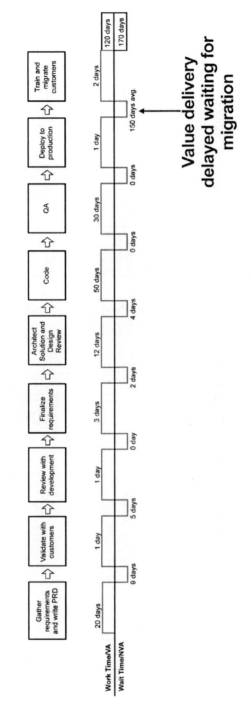

Figure 8.1: Value Stream map with long queue for customer migration

Process Cycle Efficiency = 22 days/23 days = 96%

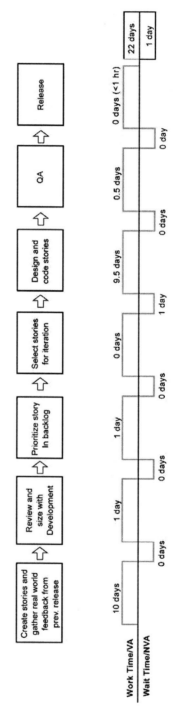

Figure 8.2: Value Stream map for Agile project with little wait time

Perceived integrity refers to the total product's ability to delight the customer by striking the perfect balance of capability, usability, quality (or reliability), and value. Perceived integrity is achieved when information flows effectively between the customer and subject matter experts such as the product manager and the product team (*e.g.*, developers, designers, and testers). One of my favorite products of all time is SnagIT by TechSmith, which I use for screen captures and simple image editing. It is very powerful, easy to use, works amazingly well, and yet it only costs $45. For me, this product has high perceptual integrity.

Conceptual integrity refers to how well the system's central components work together as a cohesive whole. Thus, the architecture strikes the perfect balance between flexibility, maintainability, efficiency and responsiveness. Conceptual integrity is achieved when information flows effectively within the product team. Although I like Visio, for me it has low conceptual integrity as part of Microsoft Office. In Visio, when I select an object, such as a rectangle, I must drag it to the workspace and then size it. In PowerPoint, I click on the object and then draw it in the workspace. Similarly, in Visio, I have to highlight the text icon before I can add text to a shape. With PowerPoint, I highlight the object and start typing. These are small issues, but it is clear that Visio's presentation layer behaves differently—and is thus architected differently—from the other Office applications. The cohesiveness of the applications in Microsoft Office is missing when Visio is included in the suite. On the flip side, Word, Excel, and PowerPoint truly seem like a cohesive whole and I am able to switch between them fluidly.

Because product integrity depends heavily on information flow, achieving high integrity with traditional sequential development is challenging. You cannot just throw the product requirements over the proverbial wall and expect a great product to come back. You need to release partial information early and often between the customer and team members before everything is known, in order to shorten feedback cycles and keep everyone aligned. When building software applications using traditional sequential development, I learned to rely on a technique called "peeling the onion." I would involve development from the beginning of the product definition phase when I did not have a product requirements document drafted, and when I certainly did not know everything yet about what the product would need to do. We would iterate the requirements based on feedback from the customer and early guidance from the development team. This was my coping strategy for building integrity into a process that did not inherently support it. Agile's use of small iterations and deep communications between team members and the customer makes it a lot easier and natural to build integrity in.

See the Whole

"See the whole" looks to apply systems thinking in order to deliver value to the customer as fast as possible. It focuses the team on optimizing the whole product process instead of individual areas. For example, optimizing one area, such as coding, does not necessarily optimize cycle time for the product. If QA is backed up with more to test than it can handle, queuing theory suggests it is preferable to have developers and product managers assist with testing. The goal is to minimize cycle time and maximize delivered value, rather than maximize the utilization of a given resource, even a dear one such as development.

Optimizing the whole has a big implication to measurement. First, focus on information measurements, such as bug count, rather than performance measurements, such as bug count by developer. Performance measurements focus blame on individuals. In addition to punishing people for outcomes that are often not in their control, it further creates the illusion that the cause has been identified. This can prevent the team from searching for the actual root causes of the problem, such as how the bug was introduced into the system.

Secondly, avoid measuring disaggregated components, because that will lead to optimizing the parts rather than the whole. Measure one level higher than you would immediately think. Instead of measuring cost, schedule, and scope—because all three are important to a successful product-measure customer satisfaction, business case realization (for the company or customer), and cycle time, such as product concept to launch. Using this same reasoning, measure one level above an employee's direct contribution. Thus, the whole product team should be measured on the success of the product, rather than on their individual area of contribution. Aggregated measures align team members across different departments to optimize value delivered to the customer.

Other Lean Principles

The remaining four Lean principles have largely been covered in the general discussion of Agile. The descriptions will be kept brief.

Decide as late as possible. The goal of deciding as late as possible is to delay decision making until "the last responsible moment"[22] when you have the most information available. A good test for product managers is if defined require-

---

22. I was introduced to this term in *Lean Software Development: An Agile Toolkit* by Mary and Tom Poppendieck, and it captures the essence of balancing thoughtful action, just-in-time delivery, and risk management. The authors attribute the term to the Lean Construction Institute (http://www.leanconstruction.org)

ments change frequently, they are being specified too early. If the team is unable to estimate accurately, or excessive requirements are emerging during development or acceptance testing, they are being specified too late. Sharing partial information, be it requirements, design, or code, and communicating fully with your co-workers to iterate and evolve the solution, is key to making Lean and Agile succeed.

Deliver as fast as possible. This complements "decide as late as possible" because the faster you deliver, the later you can decide or commit to what to build next. Further, waste hides in partially-done work, and delivering as fast as possible eliminates waste. Queuing theory suggests the most efficient way to process work is by having the frequent arrival of small batches that move through the system at a steady rate. Basically, the bigger the queues, the bigger the variability in processing and the longer the cycle time of the system; thus, the longer it will take to move a requirement from idea to deployed. The Kanban card system has been adapted from manufacturing and is used to queue work and visually make it easy to see each requirements stage in the process. Figure 8.3 in the next section shows a Lean task board.

Amplify Learning. This ties into the discussion in Chapter 1 on the difference between *defined* and *empirical* processes and rapid feedback cycles. Software development is an empirical process, much like new product development. The team cycles between problem and solution as it navigates its way to the optimal answer. Iterative development increases the frequency of the learning cycles, and thus amplifies learning, allowing the team to create better solutions, faster.

Empower the team. Agile methods all deal with teams making and delivering on their own commitments. As product managers, our job is to set the direction, make clear the business case, and frame the problem. We must then be willing to step back and trust the team to develop the solution.

Product Management's Role in Defining Value

Lean defines value from the perspective of the customer because customers sustain businesses for the long term. Value is further viewed in the context of a specific product or service satisfying a customer's need at an exact price and point in time. Uncovering value requires a dedicated product team that is willing to look beyond existing products and beliefs about core competencies and enter into a dialogue with the customer to understand how that customer perceives value.[23] Leading this effort to understand the customer is the responsibility of product management. If this is not done well, the development team

---

23. James P. Womack and Daniel T. Jones, *Lean Thinking: Banish Waste and Create Wealth in Your Corporation* (New York: Free Press, 2003), 16–19.

will optimize the delivery of new features, but miss the opportunity to redefine the value equation for the customer. Moreover, value innovation often occurs in new services wrapped around the product rather than the product itself.

Lean Software Development principles take on new meaning for product management. For example, "see the whole" is not just about optimizing value delivery in the product process, but optimizing value delivery for the customer. Mapping the customers' value stream can deliver new insights on where waste exists outside your company's products. This exercise lets you understand how your products fit into your customers' Value Stream. It may further reveal new product ideas or opportunities to collaborate with your customers' suppliers to increase the value you deliver to the customer.

Lean in Practice

Lean does away with the iteration and maintains a laser focus on cycle time, throughput, and eliminating waste. Because there is no time box, Lean permits a continuous flow of requirements through the system. Corey Ladas, author of the book 'Scrumban'[24] has scaled Lean to teams as large as fifty members and provided the task board pictured in Figure 8.3. The green cards on the left are functional requirements, representing a small functional specification and test specification. The yellow cards to the right are features of the functional requirement small enough to be coded in a few days. The goal is to maximize throughput by adjusting bandwidth, thus how much is in each queue vertically, and latency, which is how long it takes to move a ticket horizontally from start to finish.

Lean planning occurs just in time as a new requirement moves into the queue, or at a regular interval while there is still work in progress. For the product manager, when a green requirements card is moved from the left hand proposed column to the adjacent analysis column, this is the pull signal to add another proposed feature. In this example, five requirements are allowed to be in the queue at any time.

---

24. Corey Ladas, *Scrumban-Essays on Kanban Systems for Lean Software Development* (Seattle: Modus Cooperandi Press, 2008).

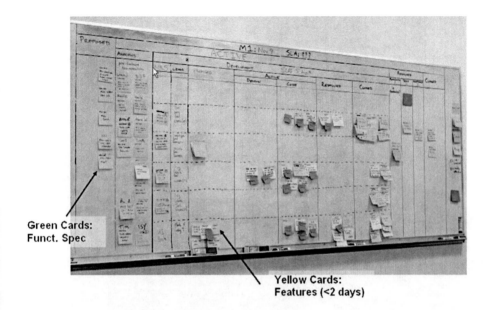

Green Cards:
Funct. Spec

Yellow Cards:
Features (<2 days)

Figure 8.3: Lean Kanban board

With a continuous flow system, an interesting idea emerges: requirements do not need to be sized because all you need to know for proper planning is the average size and the team's throughput. Tracking is done using a cumulative flow diagram (CFD) instead of a burndown chart. The CFD (Figure 8.4) shows the state of each requirement from backlog to done. Similarly, some XP teams split stories until they are all at a small and workable length. They also do away with estimating and just count stories per iteration (instead of story points) to gauge their velocity. These methods work well for the development teams, especially those that struggle with estimating, but risk short-circuiting the feedback loop with product management about the cost benefits of each feature. If your team applies one of these strategies, you need to make the expected development effort and alternative approaches an explicit point of discussion when reviewing stories with the engineering team.

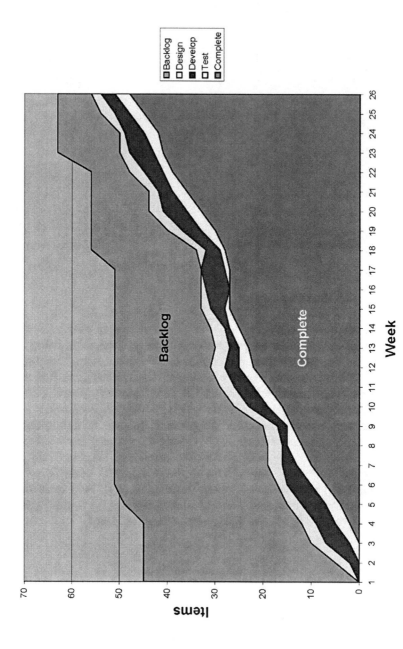

Figure 8.4: Cumulative Flow Diagram

9 | Conclusion

The foundation for Agile success has been laid down. You should now understand how Agile development works and what it requires of product managers. This final chapter looks to provide additional context around Agile and reviews the most important lessons from the book.

Process Maturity and Agile

CMMI, or the Capability Maturity Model Integration process, is a best practices process model for software development from the Software Engineering Institute at Carnegie Mellon University. It has five stages that define a company's process maturity (Figure 9.1). The first, or least mature, stage is *ad hoc*. Many start-ups fall here, as do some larger companies. The *ad hoc* stage is defined by an unpredictable environment, a reactionary mentality, and heroics by team members to achieve success. Stage two companies are more advanced, incorporating requirements managements and quality assurance. Although this is a big step forward, stage two companies still tend to be reactionary. By stage three, a company has defined its process across projects and is managing multiple interdependent projects. Companies at this stage usually have products that share a common platform and components. Further, in addition to QA, the company performs actual validation of user requirements (*i.e.*, acceptance testing with customers). By stage four there is significant measurement or instrumentation of processes, and by stage five the company systematically follows a standard process for continuous improvement.

Process Maturity and Agile

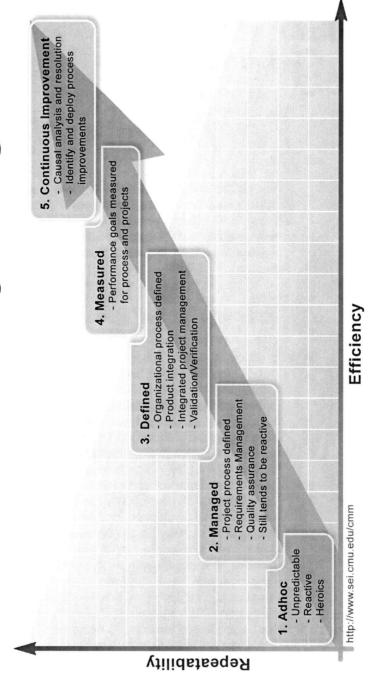

Figure 9.1: *CMMI Process Maturity Model*

Companies that implement CMMI can be guilty of valuing process over individuals. There is a legitimate concern that when process or, even worse, certification becomes the goal, a situation similar to that which happened with ISO 9000 can occur. ISO 9000 is a quality management standard. ISO Certification, however, does not ensure a high quality, or perceived integrity, from the customer perspective. It simply proves that a company has fully documented its systems and processes and can produce its product consistently and without variation.

Not surprisingly, there has been much debate over the compatibility of CMMI with Agile. The Agile camp feels CMMI is too rigid and process-driven, and the CMMI camp believes Agile is too *ad hoc*. Nevertheless, there is a lot more common ground than there are differences. Most importantly, Agile methods are not *ad hoc*, but well-designed processes optimized to accommodate uncertainty. The biggest area where some of the methods like XP do fall down in CMMI's view is around written documentation, because most of the documentation in XP is either oral communication or documentation through code. These shortcomings, if you view them as such, can be mitigated through the use of software tools to capture stories and provide traceability for acceptance testing.

Companies using CMMI should still be able to make it work effectively with Agile development. Systematic, a five-hundred-person independent software and systems company, uses CMMI for planning and tracking at the project level and Agile for planning and tracking at the iteration level. The Product Backlog acts as their interface between CMMI and Agile. The Sprint Review provides the feedback for the project-level tracking. Systematic introduced a fifteen minute risk management meeting, scheduled every two weeks, to report status on known risks and identify any new risks. They also have set definitions and checklists demonstrating DONE for the Sprint and READY for stories in the product backlog. The Product Owner is responsible for ensuring that stories in the Product Backlog that are READY do not fall below 110 percent of the current velocity.[25] Following CMMI may add additional overhead to Agile, but may also deliver additional efficiencies in process improvement and repeatability.

---

25. Carsten Ruseng Jakobsen and Jeff Sutherland. "Mature Scrum at Systematic," *Methods and Tools* 17, no. 3 (Fall 2009): 2–14.

Sweet Spots for Agile Development

I am frequently asked about which Agile methods are optimal for different types of products and projects. I dread this question and do my best to avoid answering it because it is dependent on so many variables, including product type, stage in lifecycle, business culture, regulation, and team member skills and personalities. Further, the methods cannot be directly compared. It is similar to comparing apples to oranges. XP says a lot about how to go about developing, such as pair programming, coding standards and so on, whereas Scrum is much more a project management methodology that can be widely applied to different development strategies. Likewise, ASD or Adaptive Software Development has been described as an approach and attitude over a method.[26] It is therefore challenging to make a straightforward recommendation.

Companies have scaled and adapted XP to large teams of around one hundred, and Scrum into the multiple hundreds. These boundaries are fluid, and aspects of each get traded off based on the problem. Please consider the table in Figure 9.2 as a rough guide and starting point for exploring some of the different Agile methods. It is a gross simplification and many counterpoints exist. Still, if you were wondering which methods might be best suited for your situation, I am hopeful that you will find this table instructive in understanding each method's "sweet spot" and where each might work best.

Organizational Agility Trade-Offs

Agile is a logical choice for projects that are small, rapidly changing, and have rapid release cycles. Many web services are perfect examples. As projects become larger, there are more developers and more interfaces and dependencies with other groups and systems. The team is usually also more distributed. This added complexity starts favoring increased periods of definition and upfront planning, as well as end-of-project testing and validation.

- If your market is regulated, or if your products work in mission-critical environments, you will need to generate more documentation, perform more thorough testing, have formal check-offs, and support change control and traceability.

---

26. M. A. Awad, "A Comparison between Agile and Traditional Software Development Methodologies," (PhD diss., University of Western Australia, 2005), 15.

Sweet Spots

	Team	Complexity/dependencies	Requirements	Culture	Time to Market
XP	small	low to medium	dynamic	empowered	fast
Scrum/Lean	small to medium	medium	dynamic	empowered	fast
FDD	medium to large	medium/high	moderate changes	empowered	medium
AUP	medium to large	high	moderate changes	Command & Control	medium/long
Traditional	large	high	stable	Command & Control	long

Disclaimer: *this is a gross simplification*

Figure 9.2: Comparison of different Agile methods

- If you work in a high command and control culture, management is going to want all of the above items as well as the perceived project control of Gantt charts. Showing them regular increments of working software may persuade them that the Gantt chart is not adding value, but do not count on it.

- If your products go into other companies' products, such as chipsets, you will need to commit to more definition upfront because your customers are performing parallel development.

- If it makes economic sense to fully define the architecture up front because rework will truly be expensive, the traditional model would be favored, recognizing the cost of delaying time to market and accommodating change.

- If you deal with large, difficult customers requiring customized development and there is little trust between parties, you probably need to specify everything up front. This will favor traditional development, at least in the definition stage and will come at the expense of customer and user satisfaction.

Ultimately, you need to decide what is right for your project, your company, and your team's skill set. Strike the balance that will let you deliver the most value to your customers with the maximum efficiency. Determine where you need to be on the Agile/Traditional spectrum in Figure 9.3 and how Agile you desire to be. Regardless of where you start, continually question your assumptions about how much definition you really need to start developing the solution, how to push out decisions to the last responsible moment when you will have the best information available, and how to keep yourself flexible to accommodate the dynamic marketplace in which you work and compete.

Organizational Agility Tradeoffs

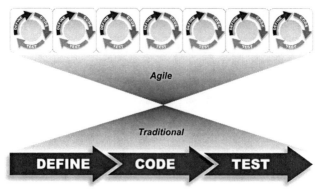

Figure 9.3: Organizational agility trade-offs

Agile Product Management Review

Let's do a quick review to summarize how all the pieces fit together for successful Agile product management:

1. Regardless of development methodology, you have to have a sound product strategy feeding your roadmap. Once the strategy is in place, lay out the roadmap to show how you are going to achieve your product vision.

2. Split the roadmap into releases and build the Product Backlog, adding more detail to requirements towards the top, or about sixty to ninety days out. If your detailed roadmap has twelve months because you have a longer release cycle product, only forecast backlog for about 70 percent of your expected velocity and reserve 30 percent to accommodate changes and uncertainty. By doing this, you will avoid disappointing your constituents by having to remove something that they considered important.

3. Map the Product Backlog to Sprints and Sprints to releases. Work with your development team at the beginning of each iteration to finalize the content and set the goal for the Sprint. Further, revisit your product strategy at least quarterly and your roadmap monthly. These are living documents.

4. Once you have successfully completed your first Sprint, develop your rhythm to work across about one hundred and twenty days of iterations. If you practice thirty-day Sprints, you would work across four iterations concurrently. Thus, two iterations back, gather feedback from customers about upcoming features and priorities. One iteration back, validate designs with your customers. On the current iteration, be available to support the development team, and on the iteration that just finished, validate the working software with your customers. Remember to have a few evergreen features in the product backlog. These are important features that are technically difficult but require little or no input from the product management team. Evergreen features are good to have just in case you experience a Product Backlog item that takes longer than expected to have its details finalized.

Leverage all of the Agile tools (Figure 9.4). The Product Backlog is not just a prioritized list of requirements, but also a great way to communicate your priorities to the team and other stakeholders. Capture requirements as user stories, which are placeholders for conversations with the development team and are easy to reprioritize with each iteration. Use velocity to track how many stories were completed and to plan the next iteration. Use burndown charts of story points and task hours to track and adjust the release and each iteration. Periodically, spend an hour creating a Value Stream map to identify areas for organizational improvement within product management, development, and the deployment process. In particular, look for constraints that show up around hand-offs, approvals, QA, and documentation.

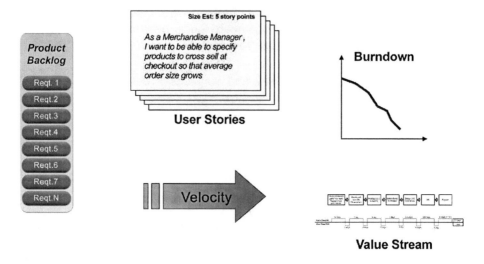

Figure 9.4: Agile tools for the product manager

Leadership

The mechanics of Agile product management, which are covered in this book, need to be understood. But the single most important piece of advice I can give on how to be successful has nothing to do with Agile. It is to remember to lead. The biggest complaint I hear from Agile developers about product managers (and Product Owners) is that they are not leading and setting the vision. In other words, it is not that the requirements are too vague or important acceptance tests were missed, it is that the product manager is failing to lead convincingly and with conviction. So how does one lead?

Have a vision and roadmap—Always reiterate the big picture to keep the team and stakeholders focused on the goal and prioritizing correctly. Everyone on the team should know the big picture objective.

Be the expert on your customers, your market, your product, and how your development team builds software[27]—you are the go-to person for these areas and it means you will need to spend time in the field and with customers to develop this expertise. This will present a challenge when it comes to being always available to the team, and you will have to balance this. But if you are not an expert, you will not be that valuable to the team anyway. Thus, it is better to be a little harder to reach and have something worthwhile to contribute than the opposite.

Make the tough trade-offs—Part of leading is making tough decision that no one else wants to make or should be making. These must be informed decisions, and you need to build understanding with the team and your stakeholders around your decisions so they are respected. You want to avoid being or being viewed as arbitrary. But your job is to balance competing priorities and that requires making tough calls. You cannot always please everyone. On the positive side, with Agile, you can offer your constituents much more flexibility and make decisions with better information.

Protect the team—Protect the team from interference and enforce respect for the iteration. You own the Product Backlog and priorities. If stakeholders disagree with the team's work plan, they should not be doing an end run. They need to go through you. Agile accommodates a release having scope creep, but an iteration should not. Avoid the temptation. Lastly, spread credit for successes and take responsibility for failures. This will earn you the respect and loyalty of the team.

Act with integrity—This should be self-explanatory and needs no further amplification other than to say Agile demands strong trust between team members. If you are not trusted to be straight with the team, you will have a hard time being successful. This advice extends to your entire business career and personal life.

Motivate those around you—Be passionate. Be enthusiastic. Be hard working. The Product Backlog will not motivate your team. You need to paint the picture of *why* they should be motivated. You also need to know when to step back. Your job is to establish the vision and set the objective for the team. You want to give the team the problem to be solved, and then give them the freedom to solve it.

Leading well is the single most important thing you can do to be a successful product manager with Agile.

---

27. Ivon Chong, "Leadership in Product Management" (paper presented at the monthly meeting for Silicon Valley Product Management Association, May 7, 2003).

Visibility, Flexibility, and Quality

In closing, I wanted to reiterate why Agile is good for product management. Agile provides clear **visibility** into the progress of each release with story points, velocity, and burndown charts, plus frequent delivery of working software. Agile ensures product quality with automated unit tests, ideally written prior to coding, acceptance testing against user criteria, and early validation with customers. Furthermore, the time devoted to bug fixing decreases, allowing more resources to be devoted to new development. Lastly, Agile delivers a new **flexibility** to be able to reprioritize before each iteration throughout the release cycle. We can easily incorporate new requirements and customers' needs as they emerge and make more informed decisions.

This book should in no way be the end of your Agile education. Take advantage of the many resources available, some of which are listed in the appendix. Best practices are still emerging, and Agile needs to be tuned to each situation. Refer to the Agile Excellence Product Management Framework (Figure 9.5) to stay focused on being a good leader, remind you of Agile's guiding principles, and keep sight of how to move between strategic and tactical activities to deliver successful products to the marketplace. A full-size version, as well as additional materials and templates, can be downloaded at http://www.agile-excellence.com. Once at the website, hover over "Book" on the navigational menu and select "Reader Only Resources" from the submenu. The user name is "reader" and the password is "success" (all lowercase and without the quotation marks). Enter these to unlock this bonus material. You are now well on your way to achieving Agile Excellence. Enjoy the journey.

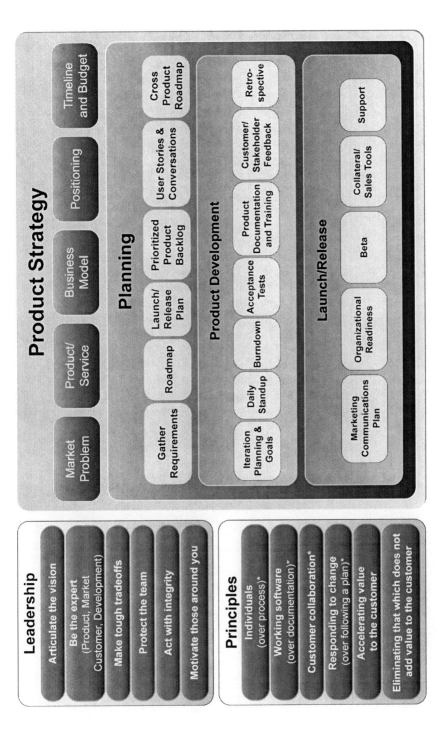

Figure 9.5: Agile product management framework

A Glossary

- **Acceptance Tests**—Tests that confirm the software meets the user's criteria and satisfies the business need.

- **Burndown Charts**—Charts that show how much work remains to be completed in the iteration or release tracked against time. For example, a release burndown chart maps Story Points, or similar metric, remaining in the release at the start of each iteration in the release. An iteration or Sprint burndown chart shows how many task hours remain at the start of each day in the iteration.

- **Constraint Card**—A method developed by Mike Cohn of Mountain Goat Software to capture constraint requirements. Seven constraints are covered: performance, accuracy, portability, reusability, maintainability, interoperability, and capacity. Constraint requirements take a different form because they are difficult to fully communicate in the user story format.

- **Daily Standup (Daily Scrum)**—A daily status meeting for the Agile development team to synchronize and coordinate effort. The meeting lasts approximately fifteen minutes. Each member takes a turn answering three questions: what she accomplished yesterday, what she plans to accomplish today, and whether she has encountered any obstacles.

- **Extreme Programming (XP)**—A lightweight Agile development methodology developed by Kent Beck in 1996 to deliver value quickly in the face of vague and rapidly changing requirements.

- **Grooming the Product Backlog**—The process of updating and enhancing the Product Backlog, including adding new requirements (or stories), reprioritizing requirements, adding detail to requirements, and dividing large requirements into smaller ones.

- **Iteration (Sprint)**—An iteration or Sprint is a time-boxed period, usually lasting one to four weeks, which sets the team's cadence and includes definition, coding, and testing. The deliverable at the end of each iteration (except iteration zero) is working software that is ideally potentially shippable. Scrum defines four stages of the Sprint: planning, development, review, and the retrospective.

- **Iteration Zero**—Iteration zero occurs when starting a project to allow the development environment to be set up, the story cards for the Product Backlog to be written, and UI and prototypes to be tested. It is different from the standard iteration in that working software is not delivered.

- **Kanban**—Used in Lean Software Development and adapted from Lean Manufacturing, Kanban is a signaling system, historically based around cards, to indicate demand for an item. Kanban is used to reduce inventory queues and work in progress (WIP). In manufacturing, the cards represent requests for parts needed for the next batch of work. In software the card represents a unit of work, such as a feature. As the card moves through the different stages of the task board, its removal from one stage or queue is the signal to add the next item. For example, product management might be allowed to have five features in queue to be developed. When a developer takes a feature from the queue to start design work, it leaves an empty slot. The product manager, upon seeing only four features in the queue, would then add the next feature from the Product Backlog.

- **Lean Software Development**—An Agile development methodology adapted by Mary and Tom Poppendieck from Toyota's Lean Manufacturing philosophies. There are seven principles, the most important being to eliminate waste, which includes work in progress (any work not yet released to the customer), extra processes, waits, defects, etc.

- **Minimum Marketable Feature (MMF)**—The minimum capabilities that must be developed so the feature is both useful and usable by the user. MMF is an important concept in splitting requirements for development and defining releases.

- **Planning Game**—One of XP's twelve core practices that is used to set the scope of next release by balancing business priorities and technical estimates. The product manager decides the priorities and balances scope and dates while development owns estimates, process, technical consequences, and detailed scheduling of the development.

- **Planning Meeting (Sprint Planning)**—This meeting is used to kick off an iteration. The product manager or Product Owner facilitates the meeting to set the goal for the iteration, make any final adjustments to the Product Backlog prioritization, and determine which requirements will be built based on the priority, size estimates, and the team's velocity. In Scrum, a second planning meeting is held to discuss how the requirements will be developed.

- **Product Backlog**—A list of requirements and features, often written as user stories, prioritized by business value. The Product Backlog is maintained by the product manager or Product Owner.

- **Product Owner**—The Product Owner represents the customer on a Scrum Team. He manages the Product Backlog, in particular the prioritization of requirements, and is available to the team to answer questions. He facilitates the Sprint Planning meeting and goal setting. He is also responsible for making the Product Backlog visible within the organization.

- **Product Requirements Document (PRD)**—A traditional product management document capturing the requirements for a product release, including project goals, timeline, assumptions, constraints (*e.g.*, compatibility, security, and scalability), assumptions, open issues, etc.

- **Product Roadmap**—See **Roadmap**.

- **Product Strategy**—The product strategy sets the direction of the product. It encompasses the product vision and includes the market problem and opportunity, a description of the product or service, the business model, the product positioning, and timeline and budget.

- **Product Vision**—The highest level of strategy that is easy to articulate and covers the target customer, their pain point, and how the solution will evolve to solve it.

- **Release**—A fully tested, documented, and supported version of the product that may include multiple iterations of work that is put into production or available for customers to install.

- **Release Plan**—The release plan provides an overview of the release and identifies the coordinated efforts required to make the release successful. It should include the theme of the release and key features, schedule of key milestones, responsibilities and owners, dependencies, messaging, risks and mitigations, goals, and success measures. If the release is a major marketable event, launch activities would be included.

- **Release Planning**—Release planning is a multi-step process to determine what requirements will be included in each release. It starts with taking the product roadmap and dividing it into releases (if the roadmap does not already have this level of detail); creating the corresponding Product Backlog for at least the current release; and then mapping the Product Backlog to the release through iterations. Release planning takes into account major themes, minimum functionality required, critical dates, and the market's ability to absorb new functionality.

- **Retrospective Meeting (Sprint Retrospective)**—The team meets after each iteration to review what went well and what could be improved with the goal of continually identifying better ways to work.

- **Review Meeting (Sprint Review)**—An informational meeting after each iteration for the team to demonstrate to stakeholders what was built during the last iteration. This meeting highlights what was accomplished during the iteration and provides the necessary context for the next planning meeting.

- **Roadmap**—There are many different types of roadmaps used by product managers. The most common is the Product Roadmap that covers when in time a given feature or capability will be available in the product. Other types of roadmaps include cross-product, technology, market rhythm (*e.g.*, the release cycle for Intuit's TurboTax® product is driven by the tax season), and competitive. This book concerns itself with product and cross-product roadmaps.

- **Scrum**—An Agile method developed by Jeff Sutherland, Ken Schwaber, Mike Beedle and others. Requirements are maintained in a prioritized list known as the Product Backlog and the work is accomplished in short define, code, and test iterations known as Sprints. Each Sprint has four stages: planning, development, review, and retrospective. The work is completed by a self-organizing team that includes a Product Owner and a Scrum Master.

- **Scrum of Scrums**—A meeting of Scrum Masters to coordinate multiple projects that are interdependent or share common resources. It is similar to the Daily Scrum (*i.e.*, daily standup) but occurs once or twice a week.

- **Scrum Master**—The Scrum Master makes decisions and removes obstacles to keep the team working at maximum productivity. The Scrum Master is responsible for planning the Sprint and running the daily standup meeting as well as the review and retrospective meetings.

- **Spike**—If the development team needs to do research to proceed (*e.g.*, explore multiple technologies, test different implementations, etc.), a spike is created. This is a time-boxed research story that is included in the iteration but does not result in working software.

- **Sprint**—See **Iteration**.

- **Sprint Backlog**—Working off the stories selected for the upcoming iteration, the development team creates the set of tasks needed to meet the requirements. This set of tasks is known as the Sprint Backlog.

- **Sprint Planning**—See **Planning Meeting**.

- **Sprint Review**—See **Review Meeting**.

- **Sprint Retrospective**—See **Retrospective Meeting**.

- **Story Card (User Story)**—Requirements are documented on story cards, which are often physical index cards to ensure brevity. The requirement should be high level with just enough detail to allow development to produce a rough estimate of its size. The story card is a placeholder for a more detailed conversation between the product manager and the developer to explore the full requirement.

- **Story Point**—The development team estimates the development effort of each story card using the relative metric of story points. Thus a 10-story-point feature is expected to take twice as long as a 5-story-point feature to develop. By counting the number of story points completed in an iteration, the team can determine its velocity.

- **System Quality Card**—A method developed by Ryan Shriver of theagileengineer.com to capture system quality requirements (*i.e.*, how well the system will perform a function).

- **Task**—The development team takes the requirements on the story cards and breaks them down into development steps to satisfy a requirement. Tasks typically represent four to sixteen hours of work.

- **Task Board**—A physical board where story and task cards are pinned up to show how work is progressing during the iteration. Story cards start in the leftmost Product Backlog column. As a card is worked on, it is moved to the coding column, then to the testing column and finally to the completed column. Virtual task boards that mimic physical task boards also exist.

- **Test Driven Development (TDD)**—A software development technique where the developer writes one or more automated tests that captures the desired new functionality and then develops the code for the functionality. When the tests pass, the developer knows the code works as intended.

- **Unit Test**—Unit tests are low-level tests written by the developers to test the code and confirm it works as expected. These tests allow the team to avoid the accumulation of defects in the code and to ensure that each iteration and new requirement does not break the system.

- **Velocity**—Velocity is a measure of the team's throughput. It is determined by counting the completed story points at the end of each iteration. Velocity is then used for planning future iterations and estimating release dates.

B Resources

The resources listed are limited to Agile topics. A list of general product management resources is available on the book's website at http://www.agile-excellence.com. Additional reader-only content is also available on the site.

1. Online Resource for Agile Excellence

http://www.agile-excellence.com

To access the **reader only content**, hover over "Book" on the navigational menu and select "Reader Only Resources" from the submenu. When prompted, enter username: *reader* and password: *success*.

Join the discussion on the Lean PM Yahoo! Group to keep up with the latest developments in applying Lean and Agile thinking to product management.

2. Websites

- http://www.agilealliance.org
- http://www.scrumalliance.org
- http://www.scrum.org
- http://www.limitedwipsociety.org/
- http://www.rallydev.com

3. Yahoo! Groups

- leanpm (discussion group for Agile Excellence)

- Agile-ANN

- Agileproductmanagement

- agile-usability

- extremeprogramming

- kanbandev

- leanagile

- scrumdevelopment

4. Books

- Beck, Kent. 'Extreme Programming Explained: Embrace Change.' Indianapolis: Addison-Wesley Professional, 2000.

- Cohn, Mike. 'Succeeding with Agile: For Agile Software Development.' Indianapolis: Addison-Wesley Professional, 2009.

- Cohn, Mike. 'User Stories Applied.' Indianapolis: Addison-Wesley Professional, 2004.

- Denne, Mark and Cleland-Huang, Jane. 'Software by Numbers: Low-Risk, High-Return Development.' New Jersey: Prentice Hall, 2003.

- Ladas, Corey. 'Scrumban—Essays on Kanban Systems for Lean Software Development.' Seattle: Modus Cooperandi Press, 2008.

- Locher, Drew A. 'Value Stream Mapping for Lean Development: A How-To Guide for Streamlining Time to Market.' New York: CRC Press, 2008.

- Pichler, Roman. 'Agile Product Management with Scrum: Creating Products that Customers Love.' Indianapolis: Addison-Wesley Professional, 2010.

- Poppendieck, Mary and Tom Poppendieck. 'Lean Software Development: An Agile Toolkit.' Indianapolis: Addison-Wesley Professional, 2003.

- Schwaber, Ken and Mike Beedle. 'Agile Software Development with Scrum.' New Jersey: Prentice Hall, 2008.

- Schwaber, Ken and Jeff Sutherland. *Scrum Guide* (November 2009), http://www.scrum.org/scrumguides.

- Shalloway, Alan, Guy Beaver, and James R. Trott. 'Lean-Agile Software Development: Achieving Enterprise Agility.' Boston: Addison-Wesley Professional, 2010.

- Womack, James P. and Daniel Jones. 'Lean Thinking: Banish Waste and Create Wealth in Your Corporation.' New York: Free Press, 2003.

About the Author

Greg Cohen is a 15-year Product Management veteran with extensive experience and knowledge of Agile development. He is a certified Scrum Master, member of the Agile Alliance and former President of the Silicon Valley Product Management Association. He has worked for venture start-ups and large companies alike, and has trained product managers from around the world on Agile development methods. As a practitioner and frequent commentator on product management issues, he has written and spoken on varied topics such as embracing Agile development, Lean product management, and recession proofing your career.

Greg earned an MBA with honor from Babson College and a Bachelor of Science in Mechanical Engineering with second major in Electrical Engineering from Tufts University.

Other Happy About® Books

Purchase these books at Happy About http://happyabout.info or at other online and physical bookstores.

Expert Product Management

This book teaches both new and seasoned Product Managers and Product Marketers powerful and effective ways to ensure they give their products the best possible chance for success.

Paperback $19.95
eBook $14.95

The Phenomenal Product Manager

This book goes beyond the basics and teaches you how to work more effectively with your teams, how to influence when you have no formal authority, how to get the most important work done in less time and how to manage and accelerate your career.

Paperback $19.00
eBook $14.00

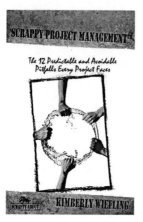

Scrappy Project Management

From the minute the project begins, all manner of changes, surprises and disasters befall them. Unfortunately most of these are PREDICTABLE and AVOIDABLE.

Paperback $19.95
eBook $14.95

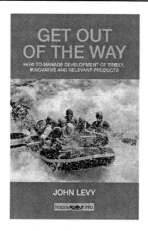

Get Out of the Way

This book offers strategies for empowering, encouraging, and directing a top-notch development team.
This book is a must have for all managers of engineering, software-development, IT, and other high-tech development organizations, as well as the executives who do business with them.

Paperback $19.95
eBook $14.95

LaVergne, TN USA
25 March 2010
177190LV00008B/1/P